THE ESSENTIAL
WISDOM OF THE
SUPREME
COURT

EDITED BY

CAROL KELLY-GANGI

FALL RIVER PRESS

New York

This book is dedicated with much love to my sister Theresa

I would like to gratefully thank all those whose support, insights, expertise, and assistance in gathering research materials made it possible for me to complete this book: Theresa A. Kelly, Esq., Christopher J. Michie, Esq., John C. Petrella, Esq., Will Petrella, and Wendy Williams. Special thanks to Catherine J. Lanctot, my former law professor from Villanova University School of Law, for graciously sharing her thoughtful insights about the Supreme Court justices.

FALL RIVER PRESS

New York

An Imprint of Sterling Publishing Co., Inc.
1166 Avenue of the Americas
New York, NY 10036

Compilation © 2019 Carol Kelly-Gangi

ISBN 978-1-4351-7001-8

Distributed in Canada by Sterling Publishing Co., Inc.
c/o Canadian Manda Group, 664 Annette Street, Toronto, Ontario M6S 2C8, Canada
Distributed in the United Kingdom by GMC Distribution Services
Castle Place, 166 High Street, Lewes, East Sussex BN7 1XU, England
Distributed in Australia by NewSouth Books
University of New South Wales, Sydney, NSW 2052, Australia

For information about custom editions, special sales, and premium and corporate purchases, please contact Sterling Special Sales at 800-805-5489 or specialsales@sterlingpublishing.com.

Manufactured in Canada

2 4 6 8 10 9 7 5 3

sterlingpublishing.com

Jacket design by David Ter-Avanesyan

CONTENTS

INTRODUCTION

* * * * *

There's no disputing that we are facing a time of deep division in the life of our nation. In these turbulent times, we can look to the justices of the Supreme Court—from the current justices to those who have served throughout history—for a measure of guidance, fortitude, and inspiration.

The Essential Wisdom of the Supreme Court gathers together hundreds of quotations from an extraordinary group of Supreme Court justices. The highest court in the nation, the Supreme Court is the "final arbiter of the law." It is tasked with ensuring that no law, state or federal, violates the Constitution, as well as ensuring that all Americans are accorded the rights that are guaranteed to them under the Constitution.

Who are the justices that are represented here? While not every justice from the history of the Court is included, the justices who have exerted the most influence over the Court and on the nation are richly represented. The selections are drawn primarily from the justices' Supreme Court opinions. In many instances, the excerpt is from the justice speaking for the Court in the majority opinion. There are also excerpts from *concurring opinions*—those opinions in which a justice agrees with some but not all of the majority opinion. Additionally, some excerpts are pulled from *dissenting opinions*—those in which a justice completely disagrees with the majority opinion. It's important to note that dissenting opinions can become the law at some later date if the Court considers the issue again, especially if the composition of the Court has changed.

Each Supreme Court justice has placed his or her own individual stamp on the Court, and the excerpts included here reflect their deeply held views on the cases that came before them as well as their own judicial philosophies. In the selections that follow, Chief Justice John Marshall emphatically proclaims a "government of laws and not of men" as paramount to American democracy. Justice Louis D. Brandeis, Justice William J. Brennan, Justice William O. Douglas, Justice Robert H. Jackson, and Justice John Paul Stevens each eloquently champion the freedom of speech that is guaranteed under the First Amendment. Justice Hugo L. Black, Justice Ruth Bader Ginsburg, Justice Anthony M. Kennedy, Justice Thurgood Marshall, and Chief Justice Earl Warren speak passionately about the equal protection of the laws guaranteed by the Constitution for every American regardless of race, ethnicity, gender, religion, or sexual orientation. Justice Stephen G. Breyer, Justice Felix Frankfurter, Justice Sandra Day O'Connor, and Chief Justice John G. Roberts explain the necessity of an independent judiciary, while Justice Harry A. Blackmun, Justice John Marshall Harlan, Justice Frank Murphy, and Justice Sonia Sotomayor each pen powerful dissents decrying racial discrimination and the enduring effects of racism.

Elsewhere, we see a more personal side of the justices. Justice Oliver Wendell Holmes writes poignantly about his grief at the passing of his wife. Justice Thurgood Marshall lovingly recalls his grandmother. Justice Elena Kagan shares her parents' quest for the American dream, and Justice David H. Souter offers a moving tribute at the passing of his dear friend, "Bill" Brennan. In a dialogue that crosses the boundaries of time and place, the justices share their keen insights on the American ideals of freedom, equality, and justice, and their solemn duty to uphold the Constitution.

The Essential Wisdom of the Supreme Court invites readers to experience the powerful words of this remarkable group of men and women who have each offered—in his or her own singular way— the guidance, leadership, and inspiration that continue to shape our great nation.

CAROL KELLY-GANGI, 2019

GOVERNMENT
AND DEMOCRACY

That the people have an original right to establish, for their future government, such principles as, in their opinion, shall most conduce to their own happiness, is the basis, on which the whole American fabric has been erected.

—**John Marshall,** *Marbury v. Madison* (1803)

The government, then, of the United States, can claim no powers which are not granted to it by the Constitution, and the powers actually granted, must be such as are expressly given, or given by necessary implication.

—**Joseph Story,** *Martin v. Hunter's Lessee* (1816)

In our complex system, presenting the rare and difficult scheme of one general government, whose action extends over the whole, but which possesses only certain enumerated powers; and of numerous State governments, which retain and exercise all powers not delegated to the Union, contests respecting power must arise.

—**John Marshall,** *Gibbons v. Ogden* (1824)

[The] government of the United States has been emphatically termed a government of laws, and not of men.

—**John Marshall,** *Marbury v. Madison* (1803)

The doctrine of the separation of powers was adopted by the Convention of 1787, not to promote efficiency but to preclude the exercise of arbitrary power. The purpose was, not to avoid friction, but, by means of the inevitable friction incident to the distribution of the governmental powers among three departments, to save the people from autocracy.

—**Louis D. Brandeis,** from his dissenting opinion in *Myers v. United States* (1926)

[E]fficiency and promptness can never be substituted for due process and adherence to the Constitution. Is not a dictatorship the most "efficient" form of government?

—**Thurgood Marshall,** dissenting opinion in *United States v. Ross* (1982)

The philosophy that constitutional limitations and legal restraints upon official action may be brushed aside upon the plea that good, perchance, may follow, finds no countenance in the American system of government.

—**George Sutherland,** *Jones v. SEC* (1936)

Decency, security and liberty alike demand that government officials shall be subjected to the same rules of conduct that are commands to the citizen. In a government of laws, existence of the government will be imperiled if it fail to observe the law scrupulously. Our Government is the potent, the omnipresent teacher. For good or for ill, it teaches the whole people by its example. Crime is contagious. If the Government becomes a lawbreaker, it breeds contempt for law; it invites every man to become a law unto himself; it invites anarchy.

> —**Louis D. Brandeis,** dissenting opinion
> in *Olmstead v. United States* (1928)

Effective self-government cannot succeed unless the people are immersed in a steady, robust, unimpeded, and uncensored flow of opinion and reporting which are continuously subjected to critique, rebuttal, and re-examination.

> —**William O. Douglas,** dissenting opinion
> in *Branzburg v. Hayes* (1972)

Whether the government treats its citizens with dignity is a question whose answer must lie in the intricate texture of daily life. Neither a judge nor an administrator who operates on the basis of reason alone can fully grasp that answer, for each is cut off from the wellspring from which concepts such as dignity, decency, and fairness flow.

> —**William J. Brennan Jr.,** from his speech "Reason,
> Passion, and the Progress of Law," presented at the
> Forty-Second Annual Benjamin N. Cardozo Lecture to
> the Association of the Bar of the City of New York, 1987

Today, as in ages past, we are not without tragic proof that the exalted power of some governments to punish manufactured crime dictatorially is the handmaid of tyranny.

—**Hugo L. Black**, *Chambers v. Florida* (1940)

Democracy rests upon two pillars; One, the principle that all men are equally entitled to life, liberty, and the pursuit of happiness; and the other, the conviction that such equal opportunity will most advance civilization.

—**Louis D. Brandeis**, from his speech "True Americanism,"
presented at Faneuil Hall, Boston, July 5, 1915

[A] democracy has the capacity—and the duty—to learn from its past mistakes; to discover and confront persisting biases; and by respectful, rationale deliberation to rise above those flaws and injustices. . . . The idea of democracy is that it can, and must, mature. Freedom embraces the right, indeed the duty, to engage in a rational, civic discourse in order to determine how best to form a consensus to shape the destiny of the Nation and its people.

—**Anthony M. Kennedy**, *Schuette v. BAMN* (2014)

The most important office and the one which all of us can and should fill is that of private citizen. The duties of the office of private citizen cannot under a republican form of government be neglected without serious injury to the public.

—**Louis D. Brandeis**, 1903

LIBERTY, FREEDOM, AND JUSTICE

Those who won our independence believed that the final end of the State was to make men free to develop their faculties, and that, in its government, the deliberative forces should prevail over the arbitrary. They valued liberty both as an end, and as a means. They believed liberty to be the secret of happiness, and courage to be the secret of liberty. They believed that freedom to think as you will and to speak as you think are means indispensable to the discovery and spread of political truth; that, without free speech and assembly, discussion would be futile; that, with them, discussion affords ordinarily adequate protection against the dissemination of noxious doctrine; that the greatest menace to freedom is an inert people; that public discussion is a political duty, and that this should be a fundamental principle of the American government.

—**Louis D. Brandeis,** concurring opinion
in *Whitney v. California* (1927)

Civil liberties had their origin and must find their ultimate guaranty in the faith of the people. If that faith should be lost, five or nine men in Washington could not long supply its want.

—**Robert H. Jackson,** concurring opinion
in *Douglas v. City of Jeanette* (1943)

Where you see wrong or inequality or injustice, speak out, because this is your country. This is your democracy. Make it. Protect it. Pass it on.

—THURGOOD MARSHALL, *from a commencement address presented at the University of Virginia, 1978*

Experience should teach us to be most on our guard to protect liberty when the Government's purposes are beneficent. Men born to freedom are naturally alert to repel invasion of their liberty by evil-minded rulers. The greatest dangers to liberty lurk in insidious encroachment by men of zeal, well-meaning but without understanding.

—**Louis D. Brandeis,** dissenting opinion
in *Olmstead v. United States* (1928)

And it requires no uncommon spirit of prophecy to foresee, that, whenever the liberties of this country are to be destroyed, the first step in the conspiracy will be to bring courts of justice into odium; and, by overawing the timid, and removing the incorruptible, to break down the last barrier between the people and universal anarchy or despotism.

—**Joseph Story,** from an address delivered before
the Suffolk Bar, Boston, September 4, 1821

There are many who talk of "protecting our liberties" as though they were gems in a safe deposit box or speak of "preserving our freedom" as though it were a pickle to be kept in brine. The fact is that liberty is a part of our law and cannot exist apart from it. Freedom is never a product of anarchy but is the child of order. It is only possible for men to be free where there is a social order that sanctions patterns of conduct which respect freedoms.

—**Robert H. Jackson,** speech upon his
acceptance of the Cardozo Memorial Award,
Washington, D.C., February 21, 1941

History teaches that grave threats to liberty often come in times of urgency, when constitutional rights seem too extravagant to endure. The World War II relocation camp cases, and the Red scare and McCarthy-era internal subversion cases, are only the most extreme reminders that, when we allow fundamental freedoms to be sacrificed in the name of real or perceived exigency, we invariably come to regret it.

—**Thurgood Marshall,** dissenting opinion in *Skinner v. Railway Labor Executives' Association* (1989)

Although the Court has not assumed to define "liberty" with any great precision, that term is not confined to mere freedom from bodily restraint. Liberty under law extends to the full range of conduct which the individual is free to pursue, and it cannot be restricted except for a proper governmental objective.

—**Earl Warren,** *Bolling v. Sharpe* (1954)

The nature of injustice is that we may not always see it in our own times. The generations that wrote and ratified the Bill of Rights and the Fourteenth Amendment did not presume to know the extent of freedom in all of its dimensions, and so they entrusted to future generations a charter protecting the right of all persons to enjoy liberty as we learn its meaning. When new insight reveals discord between the Constitution's central protections and a received legal stricture, a claim to liberty must be addressed.

—**Anthony M. Kennedy,** *Obergefell v. Hodges* (2015)

Liberty, Freedom, and Justice

It's important to every American that the law protect his or her basic liberty. We developed a system of protecting human liberty such that judges and independent judges are a necessary part of that protection. I think it's important that Americans understand that. And if that independence is seriously eroded, it will be hard to protect those things that this country was based upon.

—**Stephen G. Breyer,** from an interview with
Bill Moyers for *Frontline* on PBS, 1999

The Framers of the Constitution knew human nature as well as we do. They too had lived in dangerous days; they too knew the suffocating influence of orthodoxy and standardized thought. They weighed the compulsions for restrained speech and thought against the abuses of liberty. They chose liberty.

—**William O. Douglas,** dissenting opinion
in *Beauharnais v. Illinois* (1952)

We come from many different backgrounds, many different religions, many different ethnicities, but we have this thing called the Declaration of Independence, this document called the Constitution, in common. They define us. The best part about this job is that you can have a very small part in reminding yourself and reminding the legal system and reminding the public, that this is our heritage, our freedom.

—**Anthony M. Kennedy,** from an interview with Susan Swain
for C-SPAN, June 25, 2009; quoted from *The Supreme Court: A
C-SPAN Book Featuring the Justices in Their Own Words,* 2010

If our free society is to endure, and I know it will, those who govern must recognize that the Framers of the Constitution limited their power in order to preserve human dignity and the air of freedom which is our proudest heritage. The task of protecting these principles does not rest solely with nine Supreme Court Justices, or even with the cadre of state and federal judges. We all share the burden.

—**William J. Brennan Jr.**, in *Reason and Passion: Justice Brennan's Enduring Influence*, edited by E. Joshua Rosenkranz and Bernard Schwartz, 1997

But what is it to justice how many or how few, how high or how low, how rich or how poor, the contending parties may chance to be? Justice is indiscriminately due to all, without regard to numbers, wealth, or rank.

—**John Jay**, *Georgia v. Brailsford* (1794)

What we are seeking is not merely the justice that one receives when his rights and duties are determined by the law as it is; what we are seeking is the justice to which law in its making should conform. Justice in this sense is a concept by far more subtle and indefinite than any that is yielded by mere obedience to a rule. It remains to some extent, when all is said and done, the synonym of an aspiration, a mood of exaltation, a yearning for what is fine or high.

—**Benjamin N. Cardozo**, in *The Growth of the Law*, 1927

You sit up there, and you see the whole gamut of human nature. Even if the case being argued involves only a little fellow and $50, it involves justice. That's what is important.

> —**Earl Warren**, from an interview after his nomination to the Supreme Court, 1953

The sordid controversies of litigants are the stuff of which great and shining truths will ultimately be shaped.

> —**Benjamin N. Cardozo**, in *The Nature of the Judicial Process*, 1921

There can be no equal justice where the kind of trial a man gets depends on the amount of money he has.

> —**Hugo L. Black**, *Griffin v. Illinois* (1956)

We educated, privileged lawyers have a professional and moral duty to represent the underrepresented in our society, to ensure that justice exists for all—both legal and economic justice.

> —**Sonia Sotomayor**, from an interview with *The Hispanic Outlook in Higher Education*, 2002

When the rights of any individual or group are chipped away, the freedom of all erodes.

> —**Earl Warren**, in "The Law and the Future," *Fortune*, November 1955

Equal justice under law is not merely a caption on the facade of the Supreme Court building; it is perhaps the most inspiring ideal of our society. It is one of the ends for which our entire legal system exists . . . it is fundamental that justice should be the same, in substance and availability, without regard to economic status.

> —**Lewis F. Powell Jr.**, remarked during an address to the American Bar Association Legal Services Program, August 10, 1976

Americans have one of the greatest legal systems, but not a monopoly of the sense of justice, which is universal; nor have we a permanent copyright on the means of securing justice, for it is the spirit and not the form of law that keeps justice alive.

> —**Earl Warren**, in "The Law and the Future," *Fortune*, November 1955

Freedom and equality are not achieved overnight. Democracy takes work and time and constant effort. Liberty requires us to place ourselves in another's shoes, to see that things may not be as fair or as equitable as they appear from our own vantage points. Justice compels us to understand the rage, to feel the pain, to respond to the cries. Although it is easy to become impatient and discouraged by process failure and social discord, we must all take the long view of democratic change.

> —**Sandra Day O'Connor**, in *The Majesty of the Law: Reflections of a Supreme Court Justice*, 2003

THE LAW AND THE
RULE OF LAW

The law is the witness and external deposit of our moral life. Its history is the history of the moral development of the race.

—**Oliver Wendell Holmes Jr.**, in "The Path
of the Law," *Harvard Law Review*, 1897

[F]ragile as reason is and limited as law is as the expression of the institutionalized medium of reason, that's all we have standing between us and the tyranny of mere will and the cruelty of unbridled, undisciplined feeling.

—**Felix Frankfurter**, in "Between Us and
Tyranny," *Time*, September 7, 1962

Law matters because it keeps us safe, because it protects our most fundamental rights and freedoms, and because it is the foundation of our democracy.

—**Elena Kagan**, from the opening statement of her Senate
confirmation hearing, Washington, D.C., June 28, 2010

Law accepts as the pattern of its justice the morality of the community whose conduct it assumes to regulate.

—**Benjamin N. Cardozo**, in *The Paradoxes of Legal Science*, 1928

The life of the law has not been logic: it has been experience. The felt necessities of the time, the prevalent moral and political theories, intuitions of public policy, avowed or unconscious, even the prejudices which judges share with their fellow-men, have had a good deal more to do than the syllogism in determining the rules by which men should be governed. The law embodies the story of a nation's development through many centuries, and it cannot be dealt with as if it contained only the axioms and corollaries of a book of mathematics.

—**Oliver Wendell Holmes Jr.**, in *The Common Law*, 1881

We shall unite in viewing as law that body of principle and dogma which with a reasonable measure of probability may be predicted as the basis for judgment in pending or in future controversies.

—**Benjamin N. Cardozo**, in *The Growth of the Law*, 1927

The truth is, that the law is always approaching, and never reaching, consistency. It is forever adopting new principles from life at one end, and it always retains old ones from history at the other, which have not yet been absorbed or sloughed off. It will become entirely consistent only when it ceases to grow.

—**Oliver Wendell Holmes Jr.**, in *The Common Law*, 1881

My analysis of the judicial process comes then to this, and little more: logic, and history, and custom, and utility, and the accepted standards of right conduct, are the forces which singly or in combination shape the progress of the law.

> —**Benjamin N. Cardozo,** in *The Nature of the Legal Process,* 1921

The law is not a series of calculating machines where definitions and answers come tumbling out when the right levers are pushed.

> —**William O. Douglas,** in "The Dissent: A Safeguard of Democracy," *Journal of the American Judicature Society,* 1948

Law not served by power is an illusion; but power not ruled by law is a menace which our nuclear age cannot afford.

> —**Arthur Goldberg,** speech at Catholic University, Washington, D.C., June 1966

There can be no free society without law administered through an independent judiciary. If one man can be allowed to determine for himself what is law, every man can. That means first chaos, then tyranny. Legal process is an essential part of the democratic process.

> —**Felix Frankfurter,** concurring opinion in *United States v. United Mine Workers of America* (1947)

In the framework of our Constitution, the President's power to see that the laws are faithfully executed refutes the idea that he is to be a lawmaker. The Constitution limits his functions in the lawmaking process to the recommending of laws he thinks wise and the vetoing of laws he thinks bad. And the Constitution is neither silent nor equivocal about who shall make laws which the President is to execute. . . . The Founders of this Nation entrusted the lawmaking power to the Congress alone in both good and bad times.

—**Hugo L. Black,** *Youngstown Sheet*
& Tube Co. v. Sawyer, 1952

The search for a static security—in the law or elsewhere—is misguided. The fact is that security can only be achieved through constant change, through the wise discarding of old ideas that have outlived their usefulness, and through the adapting of others to current facts.

—**William O. Douglas,** in "Stare Decisis,"
Columbia Law Review, June 1949

It is revolting to have no better reason for a rule of law than that so it was laid down in the time of Henry IV. It is still more revolting if the grounds upon which it was laid down have vanished long since, and the rule simply persists from blind imitation of the past.

—**Oliver Wendell Holmes Jr.,** from an address delivered
at the Boston University School of Law, January 1897

[T]here is very little truth in the old refrain that one cannot legislate equality. Laws not only provide concrete benefits; they can even change the hearts of men—some men anyway—for good or for evil. . . . the hearts of men do not change of themselves.

> —**Thurgood Marshall**, from an address delivered
> at the White House for a conference titled
> "To Fulfill These Rights," June 1, 1966

If we desire respect for the law, we must first make the law respectable.

> —**Louis D. Brandeis**, quoted in *The Brandeis Guide
> to the Modern World*, edited by Alfred Lief, 1941

Future lawyers should be more aware that law is not a system of abstract logic, but the web of arrangements, rooted in history but also in hopes, for promoting to a maximum the full use of a nation's resources and talents.

> —**Felix Frankfurter**, from an address at the
> Inauguration of Dr. Harry N. Wright, College of
> the City of New York, September 30, 1942

[R]espect for judicial process is a small price to pay for the civilizing hand of law, which alone can give abiding meaning to constitutional freedom.

> —**Potter Stewart**, *Wyatt Tee Walker v.
> City of Birmingham* (1967)

It is confidence in the men and women who administer the judicial system that is the true backbone of the rule of law. Time will one day heal the wound to that confidence that will be inflicted by today's decision. One thing, however, is certain. Although we may never know with complete certainty the identity of the winner of this year's Presidential election, the identity of the loser is perfectly clear. It is the Nation's confidence in the judge as an impartial guardian of the rule of law.

—**John Paul Stevens**, dissenting
opinion in *Bush v. Gore* (2000)

We tell the new graduates that they are ready to enter a profession devoted to "those wise restraints that make us free." That phrase has always captured for me the way law, and the rule of law, matters. What the rule of law does is nothing less than to secure for each of us what our Constitution calls "the blessings of liberty"—those rights and freedoms, that promise of equality, that have defined this nation since its founding. And what the Supreme Court does is to safeguard the rule of law, through a commitment to even-handedness, principle, and restraint.

—**Elena Kagan**, from the opening statement of her Senate
confirmation hearing, Washington, D.C., June 28, 2010

The Law and the Rule of Law

The events of September 11, 2001, and thereafter shattered our peace but not our faith in our institutions. We remain persuaded of the benefits of helping to shape a world in which democratic principles predominate in national governance, and in which the Rule of Law offers the best approach to secure freedom and equality for all people. Fundamental to the Rule of Law in the United States is the role of an independent judiciary in enforcing the individual rights and liberties guaranteed by our Constitution.

—**Sandra Day O'Connor**, in *The Majesty of the Law: Reflections of a Supreme Court Justice*, 2003

I am convinced that law can be a vital engine not merely of change but of other civilizing change. That is because law, when it merits the synonym justice, is based on reason and insight. Decisional law evolves as litigants and judges develop a better understanding of the world in which we live. . . . I believe that these steps, which are the building blocks of progress, are fashioned from a great deal more than the changing views of judges over time. I believe that problems are susceptible to rational solution if we work hard at making and understanding arguments that are based on reason and experience.

—**William J. Brennan Jr.**, in "Constitutional Adjudication and the Death Penalty: A View from the Court," *Harvard Law Review*, 1986

A judge can't have any agenda. A judge can't have any preferred outcome in any particular case. And a judge certainly doesn't have a client. The judge's only obligation—and it's a solemn obligation—is to the rule of law.

> —**Samuel A. Alito Jr.**, from the opening
> statement of his Senate confirmation hearing,
> Washington, D.C., January 9, 2006

When we [Americans] talk about the rule of law, we assume that we're talking about a law that promotes freedom, that promotes justice, that promotes equality.

> —**Anthony M. Kennedy**, from an interview with American
> Bar Association President William Neukom, 2007

Every day in my work, I am reminded of the importance of civic participation. Without the general public support that interested and informed citizens provide, we would not live in a country that operates according to the rule of law.

> —**Stephen G. Breyer**, from a commencement address
> presented at The New School, May 20, 2005

THE CONSTITUTION

It is of paramount importance to me that our country has a written constitution. This great document is the unique American contribution to man's continuing search for a society in which individual liberty is secure against governmental oppression.

—**Hugo L. Black**, in *A Constitutional Faith*, 1968

A constitution is framed for ages to come, and is designed to approach immortality as nearly as human institutions can approach it. Its course cannot always be tranquil. It is exposed to storms and tempests, and its framers must be unwise statesmen indeed, if they have not provided it, so far as its nature will permit, with the means of self-preservation from the perils it may be destined to encounter.

—**John Marshall**, *Cohens v. Virginia* (1821)

If there is any principle of the Constitution that more imperatively calls for attachment than any other, it is the principle of free thought—not free thought for those who agree with us but freedom for the thought we hate.

—**Oliver Wendell Holmes Jr.**, dissenting opinion
in *United States v. Schwimmer* (1929)

A constitution, from its nature, deals in generals, not in detail. Its framers cannot perceive minute distinctions which arise in the progress of the nation, and therefore confine it to the establishment of broad and general principles.

—**John Marshall**, *Bank of United States v. Deveaux* (1809)

The constitution of the United States is to receive a reasonable interpretation of its language, and its powers, keeping in view the objects and purposes, for which those powers were conferred. By a reasonable interpretation, we mean, that in case the words are susceptible of two different senses, the one strict, the other more enlarged, that should be adopted, which is most consonant with the apparent objects and intent of the Constitution.

—**Joseph Story**, in *Commentaries on the Constitution of the United States,* 1833

But the provisions of the Constitution are not mathematical formulas having their essence in their form; they are organic living institutions transplanted from English soil. Their significance is vital, not formal; it is to be gathered not simply by taking the words and a dictionary, but by considering their origin and the line of their growth.

—**Oliver Wendell Holmes Jr.**, *Gompers v. United States* (1914)

The Constitution . . . was framed upon the theory that the peoples of the several states must sink or swim together, and that in the long run prosperity and salvation are in union and not division.

—**Benjamin N. Cardozo**, *Baldwin v. Seelig* (1935)

The Court will not pass on a constitutional question, although properly presented by the record, if there is also present some other ground on which the case may be disposed of. . . . Thus, if a case can be decided on either of two grounds, one involving a constitutional question, the other a question of statutory construction or general law, the Court will decide only the latter.

—**Louis D. Brandeis**, concurring opinion in
Ashwander v. Tennessee Valley Authority (1936)

The very purpose of a Bill of Rights was to withdraw certain subjects from the vicissitudes of political controversy, to place them beyond the reach of majorities and officials, and to establish them as legal principles to be applied by the courts. One's right to life, liberty, and property, to free speech, a free press, freedom of worship and assembly, and other fundamental rights may not be submitted to vote; they depend on the outcome of no elections.

—**Robert H. Jackson**, *West Virginia State
Board of Education v. Barnette* (1943)

One who belongs to the most vilified and persecuted minority in history is not likely to be insensible to the freedoms guaranteed by our Constitution. Were my purely personal attitude relevant, I should wholeheartedly associate myself with the general libertarian views in the Court's opinion, representing, as they do, the thought and action of a lifetime. But, as judges, we are neither Jew nor Gentile, neither Catholic nor agnostic. We owe equal attachment to the Constitution, and are equally bound by our judicial obligations whether we derive our citizenship from the earliest or the latest immigrants to these shores. As a member of this Court, I am not justified in writing my private notions of policy into the Constitution, no matter how deeply I may cherish them or how mischievous I may deem their disregard.

—**Felix Frankfurter,** dissenting opinion in *West Virginia State Board of Education v. Barnette* (1943)

The constitutional fathers, fresh from a revolution, did not forge a political strait-jacket for the generations to come.

—**Frank Murphy,** *Schneiderman v. United States* (1943)

Our Constitution was not written in the sands to be washed away by each wave of new judges blown in by each successive political wind that brings new political administrations into temporary power. Rather, our Constitution was fashioned to perpetuate liberty and justice by marking clear, explicit, and lasting constitutional boundaries for trials.

—**Hugo L. Black,** dissenting opinion in *Turner v. United States* (1970)

The Constitution

It is an inadmissibly narrow conception of American constitutional law to confine it to the words of the Constitution and to disregard the gloss which life has written upon them.

> —**Felix Frankfurter**, concurring opinion in
> *Youngstown Sheet & Tube Co. v. Sawyer* (1952)

[T]hese decisions give support to a current mistaken view of the Constitution and the constitutional function of this Court. This view, in a nutshell, is that every major social ill in this country can find its cure in some constitutional "principle," and that this Court should "take the lead" in promoting reform when other branches of government fail to act. The Constitution is not a panacea for every blot upon the public welfare, nor should this Court, ordained as a judicial body, be thought of as a general haven for reform movements.

> —**John Marshall Harlan**, dissenting
> opinion in *Reynolds v. Sims* (1964)

State constitutions, too, are a font of individual liberties, their protections often extending beyond those required by the Supreme Court's interpretation of federal law. The legal revolution which has brought federal law to the fore must not be allowed to inhibit the independent protective force of state law—for without it, the full realization of our liberties cannot be guaranteed.

> —**William J. Brennan Jr.**, in "State Constitutions and the
> Protection of Individual Rights," *Harvard Law Review*, 1977

We current Justices read the Constitution in the only way that we can: as 20th-century Americans. The genius of the Constitution rests not in any static meaning it might have had in a world that is dead and gone, but in the adaptability of its great principles to cope with current problems and current needs.

—**William J. Brennan Jr.**, from a speech
delivered at Georgetown University, 1985

[T]he Constitution will endure as a vital charter of human liberty as long as there are those with the courage to defend it, the vision to interpret it, and the fidelity to live by it.

—**William J. Brennan Jr.**, from his speech "Reason,
Passion, and the Progress of Law," presented at the
Forty-Second Annual Benjamin N. Cardozo Lecture to
the Association of the Bar of the City of New York, 1987

[I]t should go without saying that the vitality of these constitutional principles cannot be allowed to yield simply because of disagreement with them.

—**Earl Warren**, *Brown v. Board of
Education of Topeka* (1954)

The Constitution doesn't belong to a bunch of judges and lawyers. It belongs to you.

—ANTHONY M. KENNEDY, *from an interview with Academy of Achievement, 2015*

We will see that the true miracle was not the birth of the Constitution, but its life, a life nurtured through two turbulent centuries of our own making, and a life embodying much good fortune that was not. Thus, in this bicentennial year, we may not all participate in the festivities with flag-waving fervor. Some may more quietly commemorate the suffering, struggle and sacrifice that has triumphed over much of what was wrong with the original document, and observe the anniversary with hopes not realized and promises not fulfilled. I plan to celebrate the bicentennial of the Constitution as a living document, including the Bill of Rights and the other amendments protecting individual freedoms and human rights.

—**Thurgood Marshall**, from a speech delivered at
the annual seminar of the San Francisco Patent and
Trademark Law Association, Maui, Hawaii, May 6, 1987

By ensuring that no one in government has too much power, the Constitution helps protect ordinary Americans every day against abuse of power by those in authority. The Constitution gives those who serve in public office the authority they need to govern effectively, to protect Americans from the threats we face in the world today, and to promote policies to make our lives better. At the same time, the Constitution limits the power of public officials and safeguards the rights of Americans, to secure the blessings of liberty for us all.

—**John G. Roberts Jr.**, from an interview
with *Scholastic News*, 2006

I do not believe that the meaning of the Constitution was forever "fixed" at the Philadelphia Convention. Nor do I find the wisdom, foresight, and sense of justice exhibited by the Framers particularly profound. To the contrary, the government they devised was defective from the start, requiring several amendments, a civil war, and momentous social transformation to attain the system of constitutional government, and its respect for the individual freedoms and human rights, we hold as fundamental today. When contemporary Americans cite "The Constitution," they invoke a concept that is vastly different from what the Framers barely began to construct two centuries ago.

—**Thurgood Marshall**, from a speech delivered at the annual seminar of the San Francisco Patent and Trademark Law Association, Maui, Hawaii, May 6, 1987

Our Constitution is a covenant running from the first generation of Americans to us, and then to future generations. It is a coherent succession. Each generation must learn anew that the Constitution's written terms embody ideas and aspirations that must survive more ages than one. We accept our responsibility not to retreat from interpreting the full meaning of the covenant in light of all of our precedents. We invoke it once again to define the freedom guaranteed by the Constitution's own promise, the promise of liberty.

—**Sandra Day O'Connor, Anthony M. Kennedy,** and **David H. Souter,** *Planned Parenthood v. Casey* (1992)

The genius of the Constitution rests not in any static meaning it may have had in a world that is dead and gone, but in the adaptability of its great principles to cope with current problems and present needs.

> —**William J. Brennan Jr.**, from a speech delivered
> at Georgetown University, October 12, 1985

Knowledge about the ideas embodied in the Constitution and the ways in which it shapes our lives is not passed down from generation to generation through the gene pool; it must be learned anew by each generation. It is not enough simply to read or memorize the Constitution. Rather, we should try to understand the ideas that gave it life and that give it strength still today.

> —**Sandra Day O'Connor**, from remarks made at
> the Liberty Medal Award Ceremony at the National
> Constitution Center, Philadelphia, July 4, 2003

THE FIRST AMENDMENT

[T]he First Amendment does not speak equivocally. It prohibits any law "abridging the freedom of speech, or of the press." It must be taken as a command of the broadest scope that explicit language, read in the context of a liberty-loving society, will allow.

—**Hugo L. Black,** *Bridges v. California* (1941)

[W]hen men have realized that time has upset many fighting faiths, they may come to believe even more than they believe the very foundations of their own conduct that the ultimate good desired is better reached by free trade in ideas—that the best test of truth is the power of the thought to get itself accepted in the competition of the market, and that truth is the only ground upon which their wishes can safely be carried out. That, at any rate, is the theory of our Constitution.

—**Oliver Wendell Holmes Jr.,** dissenting opinion in *Abrams v. United States* (1919)

[S]peech concerning public affairs is more than self-expression; it is the essence of self-government.

—**William J. Brennan Jr.,** *Garrison v. Louisiana* (1964)

It is no longer open to doubt that the liberty of the press, and of speech, is within the liberty safeguarded by the due process clause of the Fourteenth Amendment from invasion by state action. It was found impossible to conclude that this essential personal liberty of the citizen was left unprotected by the general guaranty of fundamental rights of person and property.

—**Charles Evans Hughes**, *Near v. Minnesota* (1931)

But our society—unlike most in the world—presupposes that freedom and liberty are in a frame of reference that makes the individual, not government, the keeper of his tastes, beliefs, and ideas. That is the philosophy of the First Amendment; and it is this article of faith that sets us apart from most nations in the world.

—**William O. Douglas**, dissenting opinion in *Paris Adult Theatre I v. Slaton* (1973)

The Fathers of the Constitution were not unaware of the varied and extreme views of religious sects, of the violence of disagreement among them, and of the lack of any one religious creed on which all men would agree. They fashioned a charter of government which envisaged the widest possible toleration of conflicting views. Man's relation to his God was made no concern of the state. He was granted the right to worship as he pleased and to answer to no man for the verity of his religious views.

—**William O. Douglas**, *United States v. Ballard* (1944)

In the realm of religious faith, and in that of political belief, sharp differences arise. In both fields the tenets of one man may seem the rankest error to his neighbor. To persuade others to his own point of view, the pleader, as we know, at times resorts to exaggeration, to vilification of men who have been, or are, prominent in church or state, and even to false statement. But the people of this nation have ordained, in the light of history, that, in spite of the probability of excesses and abuses, these liberties are, in the long view, essential to enlightened opinion and right conduct on the part of the citizens of a democracy. The essential characteristic of these liberties is that, under their shield, many types of life, character, opinion and belief can develop unmolested and unobstructed. Nowhere is this shield more necessary than in our own country, for a people composed of many races and of many creeds.

—**Owen Roberts**, *Cantwell v. Connecticut* (1940)

Government in our democracy, state and national, must be neutral in matters of religious theory, doctrine, and practice. It may not be hostile to any religion or to the advocacy of no-religion, and it may not aid, foster, or promote one religion or religious theory against another or even against the militant opposite. The First Amendment mandates governmental neutrality between religion and religion, and between religion and nonreligion.

—**Abe Fortas**, *Epperson v. Arkansas* (1968)

The First Amendment expresses our Nation's fundamental commitment to religious liberty by means of two provisions—one protecting the free exercise of religion, the other barring establishment of religion. They were written by the descendants of people who had come to this land precisely so that they could practice their religion freely. Together with the other First Amendment guarantees—of free speech, a free press, and the rights to assemble and petition—the Religion Clauses were designed to safeguard the freedom of conscience and belief that those immigrants had sought. They embody an idea that was once considered radical: Free people are entitled to free and diverse thoughts, which government ought neither to constrain nor to direct.

—**Sandra Day O'Connor,** concurring opinion in
McCreary County v. American Civil Liberties Union (2005)

There is an overriding interest, I believe, in keeping the courts "out of the business of evaluating the relative merits of differing religious claims," or the sincerity with which an asserted religious belief is held. Indeed, approving some religious claims while deeming others unworthy of accommodation could be "perceived as favoring one religion over another," the very "risk the Establishment Clause was designed to preclude." The Court, I fear, has ventured into a minefield. . . .

—**Ruth Bader Ginsburg,** dissenting opinion in
Burwell v. Hobby Lobby Stores, Inc. (2014)

The First Amendment was added to the Constitution to stand as
a guarantee that neither the power nor the prestige of the Federal
Government would be used to control, support or influence the kinds
of prayer the American people can say—that the people's religions
must not be subjected to the pressures of government for change
each time a new political administration is elected to office. Under
that Amendment's prohibition against governmental establishment
of religion, as reinforced by the provisions of the Fourteenth
Amendment, government in this country, be it state or federal, is
without power to prescribe by law any particular form of prayer
which is to be used as an official prayer in carrying on any program of
governmentally sponsored religious activity.

—**Hugo L. Black,** *Engel v. Vitale* (1962)

The function of the press is very high. It is almost holy. It ought
to serve as a forum for the people, through which the people may
know freely what is going on. To misstate or suppress the news is a
breach of trust.

—**Louis D. Brandeis,** "What Public Men Think of
the Newspapers," *Collier's Weekly,* March 23, 1912

Without a free press there can be no free society. Freedom of the press,
however, is not an end in itself but a means to the end of a free society.
The scope and nature of the constitutional protection of freedom of
speech must be viewed in that light and in that light applied.

—**Felix Frankfurter,** concurring opinion
in *Pennekamp v. Florida* (1946)

[There is a] profound national commitment to the principle that debate on public issues should be uninhibited, robust, and wide-open, and that it may well include vehement, caustic, and sometimes unpleasantly sharp attacks on government and public officials.

> —**William J. Brennan Jr.,** *New York Times Co. v. Sullivan* (1964)

In the First Amendment the Founding Fathers gave the free press the protection it must have to fulfill its essential role in our democracy. The press was to serve the governed, not the governors. The Government's power to censor the press was abolished so that the press would remain forever free to censure the Government. The press was protected so that it could bare the secrets of government and inform the people. Only a free and unrestrained press can effectively expose deception in government. . . . The word "security" is a broad, vague generality whose contours should not be invoked to abrogate the fundamental law embodied in the First Amendment.

> —**Hugo L. Black,** concurring opinion in *New York Times Co. v. United States* (1971)

First Amendment freedoms are most in danger when the government seeks to control thought or to justify its laws for that impermissible end. The right to think is the beginning of freedom, and speech must be protected from the government because speech is the beginning of thought.

> —**Anthony M. Kennedy,** *Ashcroft v. Free Speech Coalition* (2002)

The First Amendment

To believe that patriotism will not flourish if patriotic ceremonies
are voluntary and spontaneous, instead of a compulsory routine, is
to make an unflattering estimate of the appeal of our institutions
to free minds. We can have intellectual individualism and the rich
cultural diversities that we owe to exceptional minds only at the price
of occasional eccentricity and abnormal attitudes. When they are so
harmless to others or to the State as those we deal with here, the price
is not too great. But freedom to differ is not limited to things that do
not matter much. That would be a mere shadow of freedom. The test
of its substance is the right to differ as to things that touch the heart
of the existing order. If there is any fixed star in our constitutional
constellation, it is that no official, high or petty, can prescribe what
shall be orthodox in politics, nationalism, religion, or other matters
of opinion, or force citizens to confess by word or act their faith
therein. . . . We think the action of the local authorities in compelling
the flag salute and pledge transcends constitutional limitations on
their power, and invades the sphere of intellect and spirit which it is
the purpose of the First Amendment to our Constitution to reserve
from all official control.

> —**Robert H. Jackson,** *West Virginia State
> Board of Education v. Barnette* (1943)

First Amendment rights, applied in light of the special characteristics
of the school environment, are available to teachers and students.
It can hardly be argued that either students or teachers shed their
constitutional rights to freedom of speech or expression at the
schoolhouse gate.

> —**Abe Fortas,** *Tinker v. Des Moines Independent
> Community School District* (1969)

The First Amendment is not so construed, however, to award merit badges for intrepid but mistaken or careless reporting. Misinformation has no merit in itself; standing alone it is as antithetical to the purposes of the First Amendment as the calculated lie. . . . The sole basis for protecting publishers who spread false information is that otherwise the truth would too often be suppressed. That innocent falsehoods are sometimes protected only to ensure access to the truth has been noted before. . . .

—**Byron White**, concurring opinion in *Ocala Star-Banner Co. v. Damron* (1971)

Our Nation is deeply committed to safeguarding academic freedom, which is of transcendent value to all of us and not merely to the teachers concerned. That freedom is therefore a special concern of the First Amendment, which does not tolerate laws that cast a pall of orthodoxy over the classroom.

—**William J. Brennan Jr.**, *Keyishian v. Board of Regents* (1967)

The Constitution says that Congress (and the States) may not abridge the right to free speech. This provision means what it says. We properly read it to permit reasonable regulation of speech-connected activities in carefully restricted circumstances. But we do not confine the permissible exercise of First Amendment rights to a telephone booth or the four corners of a pamphlet, or to supervised and ordained discussion in a school classroom.

—**Abe Fortas**, *Tinker v. Des Moines Independent Community School District* (1969)

The way to preserve the flag's special role is not to punish those who feel differently about these matters. It is to persuade them that they are wrong. . . . We do not consecrate the flag by punishing its desecration, for in doing so we dilute the freedom that this cherished emblem represents.

—**William J. Brennan Jr.**, *Texas v. Johnson* (1989)

The hard fact is that sometimes we must make decisions we do not like. We make them because they are right, right in the sense that the law and the Constitution, as we see them, compel the result. . . . Though symbols often are what we ourselves make of them, the flag is constant in expressing beliefs Americans share, beliefs in law and peace and that freedom which sustains the human spirit. The case here today forces recognition of the costs to which those beliefs commit us. It is poignant but fundamental that the flag protects those who hold it in contempt.

—**Anthony M. Kennedy**, concurring opinion in *Texas v. Johnson* (1989)

The priceless heritage of our society is the unrestricted constitutional right of each member to think as he will. Thought control is a copyright of totalitarianism, and we have no claim to it. It is not the function of our Government to keep the citizen from falling into error; it is the function of the citizen to keep the Government from falling into error. We could justify any censorship only when the censors are better shielded against error than the censored.

—**Robert H. Jackson**, concurring in part and dissenting in part in *American Communications Association v. Douds* (1950)

Those who won our independence by revolution were not cowards. They did not fear political change. They did not exalt order at the cost of liberty. To courageous, self-reliant men, with confidence in the power of free and fearless reasoning applied through the processes of popular government, no danger flowing from speech can be deemed clear and present unless the incidence of the evil apprehended is so imminent that it may befall before there is opportunity for full discussion. If there be time to expose through discussion the falsehood and fallacies, to avert the evil by the processes of education, the remedy to be applied is more speech, not enforced silence. Only an emergency can justify repression. Such must be the rule if authority is to be reconciled with freedom.

—**Louis D. Brandeis**, concurring opinion
in *Whitney v. California* (1927)

Free speech has occupied an exalted position because of the high service it has given our society. Its protection is essential to the very existence of a democracy. The airing of ideas releases pressures which otherwise might become destructive. When ideas compete in the market for acceptance, full and free discussion exposes the false, and they gain few adherents. Full and free discussion even of ideas we hate encourages the testing of our own prejudices and preconceptions. Full and free discussion keeps a society from becoming stagnant and unprepared for the stresses and strains that work to tear all civilizations apart.

—**William O. Douglas**, dissenting opinion
in *Dennis v. United States* (1951)

Fear of serious injury alone cannot justify oppression of free speech and assembly. Men feared witches and burnt women. It is the function of speech to free men from the bondage of irrational fears.

> —**Louis D. Brandeis,** concurring opinion
> in *Whitney v. California* (1927)

[T]he basis of the First Amendment is the hypothesis that speech can rebut speech, propaganda will answer propaganda, free debate of ideas will result in the wisest governmental policies. It is for this reason that this Court has recognized the inherent value of free discourse.

> —**Fred M. Vinson,** *Dennis v. United States* (1951)

I do not believe that it can be too often repeated that the freedoms of speech, press, petition and assembly guaranteed by the First Amendment must be accorded to the ideas we hate or sooner or later they will be denied to the ideas we cherish.

> —**Hugo L. Black,** from his dissenting opinion in
> *Communist Party v. Subversive Activities Control Board* (1961)

The First Amendment is often inconvenient. But that is besides the point. Inconvenience does not absolve the government of its obligation to tolerate speech.

> —**Anthony M. Kennedy,** concurring opinion in *International
> Society for Krishna Consciousness, Inc. v. Lee* (1992)

If there is a bedrock principle underlying the First Amendment, it is that the government may not prohibit the expression of an idea simply because society finds the idea itself offensive or disagreeable.

—WILLIAM J. BRENNAN JR.,
Texas v. Johnson (1989)

As a matter of constitutional tradition, in the absence of evidence to the contrary, we presume that governmental regulation of the content of speech is more likely to interfere with the free exchange of ideas than to encourage it. The interest in encouraging freedom of expression in a democratic society outweighs any theoretical but unproven benefit of censorship.

—**John Paul Stevens**, *Reno v. ACLU* (1997)

In the national debate about a serious issue, it is the expression of the minority's viewpoint that most demands the protection of the First Amendment. Whatever the better policy may be, a full and frank discussion of the costs and benefits of the attempt to prohibit the use of marijuana is far wiser than suppression of speech because it is unpopular.

—**John Paul Stevens**, *Morse v. Frederick* (2007)

That there is a social problem presented by obscenity is attested by the expression of the legislatures of the forty-eight States, as well as the Congress. To recognize the existence of a problem, however, does not require that we sustain any and all measures adopted to meet that problem. The history of the application of laws designed to suppress the obscene demonstrates convincingly that the power of government can be invoked under them against great art or literature, scientific treatises, or works exciting social controversy. Mistakes of the past prove that there is a strong countervailing interest to be considered in the freedoms guaranteed by the First and Fourteenth Amendments.

—**Earl Warren**, concurring opinion in
Roth v. United States (1957)

Whatever may be the justifications for other statutes regulating obscenity, we do not think they reach into the privacy of one's own home. If the First Amendment means anything, it means that a State has no business telling a man, sitting alone in his own house, what books he may read or what films he may watch. Our whole constitutional heritage rebels at the thought of giving government the power to control men's minds.

—**Thurgood Marshall,** *Stanley v. Georgia* (1969)

Like the course of the heavenly bodies, harmony in national life is a resultant of the struggle between contending forces. In frank expression of conflicting opinion lies the greatest promise of wisdom in governmental action; and in suppression lies ordinarily the greatest peril.

—**Louis D. Brandeis,** dissenting opinion
in *Gilbert v. Minnesota* (1920)

The dissent we witness is a reaffirmation of faith in man; it is protest against living under rules and prejudices and attitudes that produce the extremes of wealth and poverty and that make us dedicated to the destruction of people through arms, bombs, and gases, and that prepare us to think alike and be submissive objects for the regime of the computer.

—**William O. Douglas,** in *Points of Rebellion*, 1970

THE RIGHT TO PRIVACY

The present case, then, concerns a relationship lying within the zone of privacy created by several fundamental constitutional guarantees. . . . Would we allow the police to search the sacred precincts of marital bedrooms for telltale signs of the use of contraceptives? The very idea is repulsive to the notions of privacy surrounding the marriage relationship. We deal with a right of privacy older than the Bill of Rights—older than our political parties, older than our school system. Marriage is a coming together for better or for worse, hopefully enduring, and intimate to the degree of being sacred. It is an association that promotes a way of life, not causes; a harmony in living, not political faiths; a bilateral loyalty, not commercial or social projects. Yet it is an association for as noble a purpose as any involved in our prior decisions.

—**William O. Douglas**, *Griswold v. Connecticut* (1965)

If the right of privacy means anything, it is the right of the individual, married or single, to be free from unwarranted governmental intrusion into matters so fundamentally affecting a person as the decision whether to bear or beget a child.

—**William J. Brennan Jr.**, *Eisenstadt v. Baird* (1972)

The Constitution does not explicitly mention any right of privacy. In a line of decisions, however . . . the Court has recognized that a right of personal privacy, or a guarantee of certain areas or zones of privacy, does exist under the Constitution.

—**Harry A. Blackmun,** *Roe v. Wade* (1973)

Our cases long have recognized that the Constitution embodies a promise that a certain private sphere of individual liberty will be kept largely beyond the reach of government. That promise extends to women as well as to men. Few decisions are more personal and intimate, more properly private, or more basic to individual dignity and autonomy, than a woman's decision—with the guidance of her physician and within the limits specified in Roe—whether to end her pregnancy. A woman's right to make that choice freely is fundamental. Any other result, in our view, would protect inadequately a central part of the sphere of liberty that our law guarantees equally to all.

—**Harry A. Blackmun,** *Thornburgh v. American College of Obstetricians & Gynecologists* (1986)

The case does involve two adults who, with full and mutual consent from each other, engaged in sexual practices common to a homosexual lifestyle. The petitioners are entitled to respect for their private lives. The State cannot demean their existence or control their destiny by making their private sexual conduct a crime. Their right to liberty under the Due Process Clause gives them the full right to engage in their conduct without intervention of the government.

—**Anthony M. Kennedy,** *Lawrence v. Texas* (2003)

The ability of women to participate equally in the economic and social life of the Nation has been facilitated by their ability to control their reproductive lives.

—SANDRA DAY O'CONNOR, *et al.*,
*Planned Parenthood of Southeastern
Pennsylvania v. Casey* (1992)

When homosexual conduct is made criminal by the law of the State, that declaration in and of itself is an invitation to subject homosexual persons to discrimination both in the public and in the private spheres. The central holding of *Bowers* has been brought in question by this case, and it should be addressed. Its continuance as precedent demeans the lives of homosexual persons.

—**Anthony M. Kennedy,** *Lawrence v. Texas* (2003)

[B]y foreclosing all democratic outlet for the deep passions this issue arouses, by banishing the issue from the political forum that gives all participants, even the losers, the satisfaction of a fair hearing and an honest fight, by continuing the imposition of a rigid national rule instead of allowing for regional differences, the Court merely prolongs and intensifies the anguish. We should get out of this area, where we have no right to be, and where we do neither ourselves nor the country any good by remaining.

—**Antonin Scalia,** dissenting opinion in
Planned Parenthood v. Casey (1992)

We need not weigh exactly the relative strengths of these various interests. They are unquestionably important and legitimate, and Washington's ban on assisted suicide is at least reasonably related to their promotion and protection. . . . Throughout the Nation, Americans are engaged in an earnest and profound debate about the morality, legality, and practicality of physician assisted suicide. Our holding permits this debate to continue, as it should in a democratic society.

—**William H. Rehnquist,** *Washington v. Glucksberg* (1997)

DUE PROCESS AND
EQUAL PROTECTION

Whatever disagreement there may be as to the scope of the phrase "due process of law," there can be no doubt that it embraces the fundamental conception of a fair trial, with opportunity to be heard.

—**Oliver Wendell Holmes Jr.**, dissenting
opinion in *Frank v. Mangum* (1915)

[Due process], unlike some legal rules, is not a technical conception with a fixed content unrelated to time, place and circumstances. Expressing as it does in its ultimate analysis respect enforced by law for that feeling of just treatment which has been evolved through centuries of Anglo-American constitutional history and civilization, "due process" cannot be imprisoned within the treacherous limits of any formula. Representing a profound attitude of fairness between man and man, and more particularly between the individual and government, "due process" is compounded of history, reason, the past course of decisions, and stout confidence in the strength of the democratic faith which we profess.

—**Felix Frankfurter,** concurring opinion in *Joint
Anti-Fascist Refugee Committee v. McGrath* (1951)

Many controversies have raged about the cryptic and abstract words of the Due Process Clause but there can be no doubt that at a minimum they require that deprivation of life, liberty or property by adjudication be preceded by notice and opportunity for hearing appropriate to the nature of the case.

—**Robert H. Jackson,** *Mullane v. Central Hanover Bank & Trust Co.* (1950)

[A]s a generalization, it can be said that due process embodies the differing rules of fair play, which through the years, have become associated with differing types of proceedings. Whether the Constitution requires that a particular right obtain in a specific proceeding depends upon a complexity of factors. The nature of the alleged right involved, the nature of the proceeding, and the possible burden on that proceeding, are all considerations which must be taken into account.

—**Earl Warren,** *Hannah v. Larche* (1960)

We conclude that, in the field of public education, the doctrine of "separate but equal" has no place. Separate educational facilities are inherently unequal. Therefore, we hold that the plaintiffs and others similarly situated for whom the actions have been brought are, by reason of the segregation complained of, deprived of the equal protection of the laws guaranteed by the Fourteenth Amendment.

—**Earl Warren,** *Brown v. Board of Education of Topeka* (1954)

It requires no argument to show that the right to work for a living in the common occupations of the community is of the very essence of the personal freedom and opportunity that it was the purpose of the [Fourteenth] Amendment to secure. . . . If this could be refused solely upon the ground of race or nationality, the prohibition of the denial to any person of the equal protection of the laws would be a barren form of words.

—**Charles Evans Hughes,** *Traux v. Raich* (1915)

Being an obvious racial discrimination, the order deprives all those within its scope of the equal protection of the laws as guaranteed by the Fifth Amendment. It further deprives these individuals of their constitutional rights to live and work where they will, to establish a home where they choose and to move about freely. In excommunicating them without benefit of hearings, this order also deprives them of all their constitutional rights to procedural due process. Yet no reasonable relation to an "immediate, imminent, and impending" public danger is evident to support this racial restriction, which is one of the most sweeping and complete deprivations of constitutional rights in the history of this nation in the absence of martial law.

—**Frank Murphy,** dissenting opinion in
Korematsu v. United States (1944)

Equal protection does not require that all persons be dealt with identically, but it does require that a distinction made have some relevance to the purpose for which the classification is made.

—**Earl Warren,** *Baxstrom v. Herold* (1966)

Wealth, like race, creed, or color, is not germane to one's ability to participate intelligently in the electoral process.

—WILLIAM O. DOUGLAS, *Harper v. Virginia Board of Elections* (1966)

The Constitution requires that Congress treat similarly situated persons similarly, not that it engage in gestures of superficial equality.

—**William H. Rehnquist,** *Rostker v. Goldberg* (1981)

Does segregation of children in public schools solely on the basis of race, even though the physical facilities and other "tangible" factors may be equal, deprive the children of the minority group of equal educational opportunities? We believe that it does. . . . To separate them from others of similar age and qualifications solely because of their race generates a feeling of inferiority as to their status in the community that may affect their hearts and minds in a way unlikely ever to be undone.

—**Earl Warren,** *Brown v. Board of
Education of Topeka* (1954)

The arbitrary separation of citizens, on the basis of race, while they are on a public highway, is a badge of servitude wholly inconsistent with the civil freedom and the equality before the law established by the Constitution. It cannot be justified upon any legal grounds.

—**John Marshall Harlan,** the sole dissenter in *Plessy v.
Ferguson* (1896), the infamous case which upheld the doctrine
of "separate by equal" that was used to perpetuate racial
segregation until the decision in *Brown v. Board of Education*

There can be no doubt that restricting the freedom to marry solely because of racial classifications violates the central meaning of the Equal Protection Clause. These statutes also deprive the Lovings of liberty without due process of law in violation of the Due Process Clause of the Fourteenth Amendment. The freedom to marry has long been recognized as one of the vital personal rights essential to the orderly pursuit of happiness by free men. Marriage is one of the "basic civil rights of man," fundamental to our very existence and survival. . . . To deny this fundamental freedom on so unsupportable a basis as the racial classifications embodied in these statutes, classifications so directly subversive of the principle of equality at the heart of the Fourteenth Amendment, is surely to deprive all the State's citizens of liberty without due process of law. The Fourteenth Amendment requires that the freedom of choice to marry not be restricted by invidious racial discriminations. Under our Constitution, the freedom to marry, or not marry, a person of another race resides with the individual, and cannot be infringed by the State. These convictions must be reversed.

—**Earl Warren,** *Loving v. Virginia* (1967)

To give a mandatory preference to members of either sex over members of the other, merely to accomplish the elimination of hearings on the merits, is to make the very kind of arbitrary legislative choice forbidden by the Equal Protection Clause of the Fourteenth Amendment; and whatever may be said as to the positive values of avoiding intrafamily controversy, the choice in this context may not lawfully be mandated solely on the basis of sex.

—**Warren E. Burger,** *Reed v. Reed* (1971)

As in all equal protection cases. . . . the crucial question is whether there is an appropriate governmental interest suitably furthered by the differential treatment.

—**Thurgood Marshall**, et al., *Police Department of Chicago v. Mosley* (1972)

While our Constitution does not guarantee minority groups victory in the political process, it does guarantee them meaningful and equal access to that process. It guarantees that the majority may not win by stacking the political process against minority groups permanently, forcing the minority alone to surmount unique obstacles in pursuit of its goals. . . . I firmly believe that our role as judges includes policing the process of self-government and stepping in when necessary to secure the constitutional guarantee of equal protection.

—**Sonia Sotomayor**, dissenting opinion in *Schuette v. BAMN* (2014)

If everyone in this country has an opportunity to participate in his government on equal terms with everyone else, and can share in electing representatives who will be truly representative of the entire community and not some special interest, then most of the problems that we are confronted with would be solved through the political process rather than through the courts.

—**Earl Warren**, from a televised interview with the McClatchy News Service, June 25, 1969

In 1971, for the first time in our Nation's history, this Court ruled in favor of a woman who complained that her State had denied her the equal protection of its laws. . . . the Court has repeatedly recognized that neither federal nor state government acts compatibly with the equal protection principle when a law or official policy denies to women, simply because they are women, full citizenship stature— equal opportunity to aspire, achieve, participate in and contribute to society based on their individual talents and capacities.

—**Ruth Bader Ginsburg**, et al., *United States v. Virginia* (1996)

No union is more profound than marriage, for it embodies the highest ideals of love, fidelity, devotion, sacrifice, and family. In forming a marital union, two people become something greater than once they were. As some of the petitioners in these cases demonstrate, marriage embodies a love that may endure even past death. It would misunderstand these men and women to say they disrespect the idea of marriage. Their plea is that they do respect it, respect it so deeply that they seek to find its fulfillment for themselves. Their hope is not to be condemned to live in loneliness, excluded from one of civilization's oldest institutions. They ask for equal dignity in the eyes of the law. The Constitution grants them that right.

—**Anthony M. Kennedy**, *Obergefell v. Hodges* (2015)

THE RIGHTS OF
THE ACCUSED

A democratic society, in which respect for the dignity of all men is central, naturally guards against the misuse of the law enforcement process. . . . Disinterestedness in law enforcement does not alone prevent disregard of cherished liberties. Experience has therefore counseled that safeguards must be provided against the dangers of the overzealous as well as the despotic.

—**Felix Frankfurter**, *McNabb v. United States* (1943)

Under our constitutional system, courts stand against any winds that blow as havens of refuge for those who might otherwise suffer because they are helpless, weak, outnumbered, or because they are nonconforming victims of prejudice and public excitement. Due process of law, preserved for all by our Constitution, commands that no such practice as that disclosed by this record shall send any accused to his death. No higher duty, no more solemn responsibility, rests upon this Court than that of translating into living law and maintaining this constitutional shield deliberately planned and inscribed for the benefit of every human being subject to our Constitution—of whatever race, creed or persuasion.

—**Hugo L. Black**, *Chambers v. Florida* (1940), where
the Court invalidated the convictions of four black
defendants on the basis of their coerced confessions

[O]ur Government is not one of mere convenience or efficiency. It too has a stake, with every citizen, in his being afforded our historic individual protections, including those surrounding criminal trials. About them we dare not become careless or complacent when that fashion has become rampant over the earth.

—**Wiley B. Rutledge,** *Kotteakos v. United States* (1946)

To take appropriate measures in order to avert injustice even towards a member of a despised group is to enforce justice. It is not to play favorites. The boast of our criminal procedure is that it protects an accused, so far as legal procedure can, from a bias operating against such a group to which he belongs. This principle should be enforced whatever the tenets of the group—whether the old Locofocos or the Know-Nothings, the Ku Klux Klan or the Communists. This is not to coddle Communists but to respect our professions of equal justice to all.

—**Felix Frankfurter,** dissenting opinion
in *Dennis v. United States* (1950)

More is at stake than General Yamashita's fate. There could be no possible sympathy for him if he is guilty of the atrocities for which his death is sought. But there can be and should be justice administered according to law. . . . It is not too early—it is never too early—for the nation steadfastly to follow its great constitutional traditions, none older or more universally protective against unbridled power than due process of law in the trial and punishment of men—that is, of all men, whether citizens, aliens, alien enemies, or enemy belligerents.

—**Wiley B. Rutledge,** dissenting opinion
in *In re Yamashita* (1946)

[I]n a capital case, where the defendant is unable to employ counsel and is incapable adequately of making his own defense because of ignorance, feeble mindedness, illiteracy, or the like, it is the duty of the court, whether requested or not, to assign counsel for him as a necessary requisite of due process of law. . . . To hold otherwise would be to ignore the fundamental postulate, already adverted to, that there are certain immutable principles of justice which inhere in the very idea of free government which no member of the Union may disregard.

—**George Sutherland,** *Powell v. Alabama* (1932)

The right of one charged with crime to counsel may not be deemed fundamental and essential to fair trials in some countries, but it is in ours. From the very beginning, our state and national constitutions and laws have laid great emphasis on procedural and substantive safeguards designed to assure fair trials before impartial tribunals in which every defendant stands equal before the law. This noble ideal cannot be realized if the poor man charged with crime has to face his accusers without a lawyer to assist him.

—**Hugo L. Black,** *Gideon v. Wainwright* (1963)

Every defendant is entitled to a trial in which his interests are vigorously and conscientiously advocated by an able lawyer. A proceeding in which the defendant does not receive meaningful assistance in meeting the forces of the State does not, in my opinion, constitute due process.

—**Thurgood Marshall,** dissenting opinion
in *Strickland v. Washington* (1984)

There are those who say, as did Justice (then Judge) Cardozo, that under our constitutional exclusionary doctrine "[t]he criminal is to go free because the constable has blundered." In some cases this will undoubtedly be the result. But, as was said in *Elkins*, "there is another consideration—the imperative of judicial integrity." The criminal goes free, if he must, but it is the law that sets him free. Nothing can destroy a government more quickly than its failure to observe its own laws, or worse, its disregard of the charter of its own existence. . . . Having once recognized that the right to privacy embodied in the Fourth Amendment is enforceable against the States, and that the right to be secure against rude invasions of privacy by state officers is, therefore, constitutional in origin, we can no longer permit that right to remain an empty promise. . . . Our decision, founded on reason and truth, gives to the individual no more than that which the Constitution guarantees him, to the police officer no less than that to which honest law enforcement is entitled, and, to the courts, that judicial integrity so necessary in the true administration of justice.

—**Tom C. Clark**, *Mapp v. Ohio* (1961)

The abhorrence of society to the use of involuntary confessions does not turn alone on their inherent untrustworthiness. It also turns on the deep-rooted feeling that the police must obey the law while enforcing the law; that, in the end, life and liberty can be as much endangered from illegal methods used to convict those thought to be criminals as from the actual criminals themselves.

—**Earl Warren**, *Spano v. New York* (1959)

We have had frequent occasion to point out that a search is not to be made legal by what it turns up. In law it is good or bad when it starts and does not change character from its success.

—ROBERT H. JACKSON,
United States v. Di Re (1948)

Today, then, there can be no doubt that the Fifth Amendment privilege is available outside of criminal court proceedings, and serves to protect persons in all settings in which their freedom of action is curtailed in any significant way from being compelled to incriminate themselves. We have concluded that, without proper safeguards, the process of in-custody interrogation of persons suspected or accused of crime contains inherently compelling pressures which work to undermine the individual's will to resist and to compel him to speak where he would not otherwise do so freely. In order to combat these pressures and to permit a full opportunity to exercise the privilege against self-incrimination, the accused must be adequately and effectively apprised of his rights, and the exercise of those rights must be fully honored.

—**Earl Warren,** *Miranda v. Arizona* (1966)

Honoring the presumption of innocence is often difficult; sometimes we must pay substantial social costs as a result of our commitment to the values we espouse. But at the end of the day, the presumption of innocence protects the innocent; the shortcuts we take with those whom we believe to be guilty injure only those wrongfully accused and, ultimately, ourselves.

—**Thurgood Marshall,** dissenting opinion
in *United States v. Salerno* (1987)

We hold that a defendant has the right to insist that counsel refrain from admitting guilt, even when counsel's experienced-based view is that confessing guilt offers the defendant the best chance to avoid the death penalty. Guaranteeing a defendant the right "to have the *Assistance* of Counsel for *his* defense," the Sixth Amendment so demands. With individual liberty—and, in capital cases, life—at stake, it is the defendant's prerogative, not counsel's, to decide on the objective of his defense: to admit guilt in the hope of gaining mercy at the sentencing stage, or to maintain his innocence, leaving it to the State to prove his guilt beyond a reasonable doubt.

—**Ruth Bader Ginsburg**, *McCoy v. Louisiana* (2018)

We merely hold today that, where a police officer observes unusual conduct which leads him reasonably to conclude in light of his experience that criminal activity may be afoot and that the persons with whom he is dealing may be armed and presently dangerous, where, in the course of investigating this behavior, he identifies himself as a policeman and makes reasonable inquiries, and where nothing in the initial stages of the encounter serves to dispel his reasonable fear for his own or others' safety, he is entitled for the protection of himself and others in the area to conduct a carefully limited search of the outer clothing of such persons in an attempt to discover weapons which might be used to assault him. Such a search is a reasonable search under the Fourth Amendment, and any weapons seized may properly be introduced in evidence against the person from whom they were taken.

—**Earl Warren**, *Terry v. Ohio* (1968)

As Justice Brandeis explained in his famous dissent, the Court is obligated—as "[s]ubtler and more far-reaching means of invading privacy have become available to the Government"—to ensure that the "progress of science" does not erode Fourth Amendment protections. Here the progress of science has afforded law enforcement a powerful new tool to carry out its important responsibilities. At the same time, this tool risks Government encroachment of the sort the Framers, "after consulting the lessons of history," drafted the Fourth Amendment to prevent. We decline to grant the state unrestricted access to a wireless carrier's database of physical location information. In light of the deeply revealing nature of CSLI, its depth, breadth, and comprehensive reach, and the inescapable and automatic nature of its collection, the fact that such information is gathered by a third party does not make it any less deserving of Fourth Amendment protection. The Government's acquisition of the cell-site records here was a search under that Amendment.

—**John G. Roberts Jr.**, *Carpenter v. United States* (2018)

CRIME AND PUNISHMENT

Although it is not likely that a criminal will carefully consider the text of the law before he murders or steals, it is reasonable that a fair warning should be given to the world in language that the common world will understand, of what the law intends to do if a certain line is passed. To make the warning fair, so far as possible the line should be clear.

—**Oliver Wendell Holmes Jr.**,
McBoyle v. United States (1931)

But justice, though due to the accused, is due to the accuser also. . . . There is danger that the criminal law will be brought into contempt— that discredit will even touch the great immunities assured by the Fourteenth Amendment—if gossamer possibilities of prejudice to a defendant are to nullify a sentence pronounced by a court of competent jurisdiction in obedience to local law, and set the guilty free.

—**Benjamin N. Cardozo**, *Snyder v. Massachusetts* (1934)

Lawlessness is lawlessness. Anarchy is anarchy is anarchy. Neither race nor color nor frustration is an excuse for either lawlessness or anarchy.

—**Thurgood Marshall**, from a speech delivered at
a national convention of Alpha Phi Alpha fraternity
members, St. Louis, Missouri, August 1966

Our independent evaluation of the issue reveals no reason to disagree with the judgment of "the legislatures that have recently addressed the matter" and concluded that death is not a suitable punishment for a mentally retarded criminal. We are not persuaded that the execution of mentally retarded criminals will measurably advance the deterrent or the retributive purpose of the death penalty. Construing and applying the Eighth Amendment in the light of our "evolving standards of decency," we therefore conclude that such punishment is excessive and that the Constitution "places a substantive restriction on the State's power to take the life" of a mentally retarded offender.

—**John Paul Stevens**, *Atkins v. Virginia* (2002)

In sum, the punishment of death is inconsistent with all four principles: death is an unusually severe and degrading punishment; there is a strong probability that it is inflicted arbitrarily; its rejection by contemporary society is virtually total; and there is no reason to believe that it serves any penal purpose more effectively than the less severe punishment of imprisonment. The function of these principles is to enable a court to determine whether a punishment comports with human dignity. Death, quite simply, does not.

—**William J. Brennan Jr.**, concurring
opinion in *Furman v. Georgia* (1972)

The basic concern of *Furman* centered on those defendants who were being condemned to death capriciously and arbitrarily. . . . The new Georgia sentencing procedures, by contrast, focus the jury's attention on the particularized nature of the crime and the particularized characteristics of the individual defendant. While the jury is permitted to consider any aggravating or mitigating circumstances, it must find and identify at least one statutory aggravating factor before it may impose a penalty of death. In this way the jury's discretion is channeled. No longer can a jury wantonly and freakishly impose the death sentence; it is always circumscribed by the legislative guidelines. In addition, the review function of the Supreme Court of Georgia affords additional assurance that the concerns that prompted our decision in *Furman* are not present to any significant degree in the Georgia procedure applied here. For the reasons expressed in this opinion, we hold that the statutory system under which Gregg was sentenced to death does not violate the Constitution.

—**Potter Stewart**, et al., *Gregg v. Georgia* (1976)

And our adherence to the constitutional vision of human dignity is so strict that even after convicting a person according to these stringent standards, we demand that his dignity be infringed only to the extent appropriate to the crime and never by means of wanton infliction of pain or deprivation. I interpret the Constitution plainly to embody these fundamental values.

— **William J. Brennan Jr.**, from a speech delivered at the Georgetown University Law Center, Washington, D.C., 1985; quoted in "Law and Human Dignity: The Judicial Soul of Justice Brennan" by Stephen J. Wermiel, *William & Mary Bill of Rights Journal*, 1998

A judge sometimes must release a criminal. He doesn't like it, she doesn't like it, but the law requires it. And the context of an election in which you are "soft on crime" betrays a misunderstanding of the judicial process and a misunderstanding of the Constitution.

—ANTHONY M. KENNEDY, *from an interview with Bill Moyers for* Frontline *on PBS, 1999*

In recognizing the humanity of our fellow beings, we pay ourselves the highest tribute. We achieve "a major milestone in the long road up from barbarism" and join the approximately seventy other jurisdictions in the world which celebrate their regard for civilization and humanity by shunning capital punishment.

—**Thurgood Marshall,** concurring opinion
in *Furman v. Georgia* (1972)

I have spoken out often to decry the gross injustices in the administration of capital punishment in our country. I air my concerns once again today with the fervent hope that they reach receptive ears. When in *Gregg v. Georgia* the Supreme Court gave its seal of approval to capital punishment, this endorsement was premised on the promise that capital punishment would be administered with fairness and justice. Instead, the promise has become a cruel and empty mockery. If not remedied, the scandalous state of our present system of capital punishment will cast a pall of shame over our society for years to come. We cannot let it continue.

—**Thurgood Marshall,** remarks made at
the Annual Dinner in Honor of the Judiciary,
American Bar Association, August 6, 1990

Perhaps the whole business of the retention of the death penalty will seem to the next generation, as it seems to many even now, an anachronism too discordant to be suffered, mocking with grim reproach all our clamorous professions of the sanctity of life.

—**Benjamin N. Cardozo,** in the law
journal *Law and Literature,* 1931

I recognize a strong counterargument that favors constitutionality [of the death penalty]. We are a court. Why should we not leave the matter up to the people acting democratically through legislatures? The Constitution foresees a country that will make most important decisions democratically. Most nations that have abandoned the death penalty have done so through legislation, not judicial decision. . . . The answer is that the matters I have discussed, such as lack of reliability, the arbitrary application of a serious and irreversible punishment, individual suffering caused by long delays, and lack of penological purpose are quintessentially judicial matters. They concern the infliction—indeed the unfair, cruel, and unusual infliction—of a serious punishment upon an individual. I recognize that in 1972 this Court, in a sense, turned to Congress and the state legislatures in its search for standards that would increase the fairness and reliability of imposing a death penalty. The legislatures responded. But, in the last four decades, considerable evidence has accumulated that those responses have not worked. . . . Thus we are left with a judicial responsibility. For the reasons I have set forth in this opinion, I believe it highly likely that the death penalty violates the Eighth Amendment.

—**Stephen G. Breyer,** dissenting opinion
in *Glossip v. Gross* (2015)

The petitioners in the capital cases before the Court today renew the "standards of decency" argument, but developments during the four years since *Furman* have undercut substantially the assumptions upon which their argument rested. Despite the continuing debate, dating back to the nineteenth century, over the morality and utility of capital punishment, it is now evident that a large proportion of American society continues to regard it as an appropriate and necessary criminal sanction.

—**Potter Stewart,** et al., *Gregg v. Georgia* (1976)

AMERICA

In proportion as the United States assume a national form and a national character, so will the good of the whole be more and more an object of attention, and the government must be a weak one indeed, if it should forget that the good of the whole can only be promoted by advancing the good of each of the parts or members which compose the whole.

—**John Jay**, from *The Federalist Papers: No. 64*,
"The Power of the Senate," March 1788

From its founding the Nation's basic commitment has been to foster the dignity and wellbeing of all persons within its borders.

—**William J. Brennan Jr.**, *Goldberg v. Kelly* (1970)

The makers of our Constitution undertook to secure conditions favorable to the pursuit of happiness. They recognized the significance of man's spiritual nature, of his feelings, and of his intellect. They knew that only a part of the pain, pleasure and satisfactions of life are to be found in material things. They sought to protect Americans in their beliefs, their thoughts, their emotions and their sensations. They conferred, as against the government, the right to be let alone—the most comprehensive of rights, and the right most valued by civilized men.

—**Louis D. Brandeis**, dissenting opinion
in *Olmstead v. United States* (1928)

[L]et us not forget that many a poor immigrant comes to us from distant lands, ignorant of our language, strange in tattered clothes and with jarring manners, who is already truly American in this most important sense; who has long shared our ideals and who, oppressed and persecuted abroad, has yearned for our land of liberty and for the opportunity of abiding in the realization of its aims. What are the American ideals? They are the development of the individual for his own and the common good; the development of the individual through liberty and the attainment of the common good through democracy and social justice.

—**Louis D. Brandeis,** from his speech "True Americanism,"
presented at Faneuil Hall, Boston, July 5, 1915

Ours is a nation built on pride in sacrifice and commitment to shared values —on a willingness of our citizens to give of their time and energy for the good of the whole. . . . the simple truth is that our nation needs hardworking, innovative, dedicated people to devote their working lives to its operation and improvement. We have a great nation today because those bridge builders of the past gave of themselves in a way that really mattered.

—**Sandra Day O'Connor,** from a commencement
address presented at Stanford University, June 2004

America

I am . . . a first generation American on my father's side, barely second generation on my mother's. Neither of my parents had the means to attend college, but both taught me to love learning, to care about people, and to work hard for whatever I wanted or believed in. Their parents had the foresight to leave the old country, where Jewish ancestry and faith meant exposure to pogroms and denigration of one's human worth. What has become of me could happen only in America. Like so many others, I owe so much to the entry this Nation afforded to people yearning to breathe free.

—**Ruth Bader Ginsburg,** from the opening statement of her Senate confirmation hearing, Washington, D.C., July 20, 1993

America has believed that each race had something of peculiar value which it can contribute to the attainment of those high ideals for which it is striving. America has believed that we must not only give to the immigrant the best that we have, but must preserve for America the good that is in the immigrant and develop in him the best of which he is capable. America has believed that in differentiation, not in uniformity, lies the path of progress. It acted on this belief; it has advanced human happiness, and it has prospered.

—**Louis D. Brandeis,** from his speech "True Americanism," presented at Faneuil Hall, Boston, July 5, 1915

At a time in our history when the streets of the Nation's cities inspire fear and despair, rather than pride and hope, it is difficult to maintain objectivity and concern for our fellow citizens. But, the measure of a country's greatness is its ability to retain compassion in time of crisis. No nation in the recorded history of man has a greater tradition of revering justice and fair treatment for all its citizens in times of turmoil, confusion, and tension than ours. This is a country which stands tallest in troubled times, a country that clings to fundamental principles, cherishes its constitutional heritage, and rejects simple solutions that compromise the values that lie at the roots of our democratic system.

—**Thurgood Marshall,** dissenting opinion
in *Furman v. Georgia* (1972)

America has a deeply confused image of itself that is in perpetual tension. We are a nation that takes pride in our ethnic diversity, recognizing its importance in shaping our society and in adding richness to its existence. Yet, we simultaneously insist that we can and must function and live in a race and color-blind way that ignore these very differences that in other contexts we laud. That tension between "the melting pot and the salad bowl" . . . is being hotly debated today in national discussions about affirmative action. Many of us struggle with this tension and attempt to maintain and promote our cultural and ethnic identities in a society that is often ambivalent about how to deal with its differences.

—**Sonia Sotomayor,** from an address delivered
at the "Raising the Bar" symposium, UC
Berkeley School of Law, October 26, 2001

One of the strengths of this great country, one of the reasons we really are a symbol of light and of hope for the world, is the way in which people of different faiths, different races, different national origins, have come together and learned—not merely to tolerate one another, because I think that is too stingy a word for what we have achieved—but to respect and love one another.

—**Antonin Scalia**, in *Scalia Speaks: Reflections on Law, Faith, and Life Well Lived*, edited by Christopher J. Scalia and Edward Whelan, 2017

Though we have made huge progress, the work of perfection is scarcely done. Many stains remain. In this rich land, nearly a quarter of our children live in deep poverty, nearly half of our citizens do not vote, and we still struggle to achieve greater understanding and appreciation of each other across racial, religious, and socioeconomic lines. Yet we strive to realize the ideal—to become a more perfect union.

—**Ruth Bader Ginsburg**, from remarks made at the New-York Historical Society, April 10, 2018

Gratitude is one of the least articulate of the emotions, especially when it is deep. I can express with very limited adequacy the passionate devotion to this land that possesses millions of our people, born, like myself, under other skies, for the privilege that this country has bestowed in allowing them to partake of its fellowship.

—**Felix Frankfurter,** from a speech made during his acceptance of an award from the National Institute for Immigrant Welfare, New York City, May 11, 1933

The vision of human dignity embodied in our Constitution throughout most of its interpretive history is, at least for me, deeply moving. It is timeless. It has inspired citizens of this country and others for two centuries.

—**William J. Brennan Jr.**, from a speech
delivered at Columbia Law School, 1987

[The] government they devised was defective from the start, requiring several amendments, a civil war, and major social transformations to attain the system of constitutional government, and its respect for the freedoms and individual rights, we hold as fundamental today.

—**Thurgood Marshall**, from a speech delivered at
the annual seminar of the San Francisco Patent and
Trademark Law Association, Maui, Hawaii, May 6, 1987

THE ROLES OF THE JUDICIARY AND THE SUPREME COURT

It is emphatically the province and duty of the judicial department to say what the law is. Those who apply the rule to particular cases must, of necessity, expound and interpret that rule. If two laws conflict with each other, the courts must decide on the operation of each. . . . [T]he court must determine which of these conflicting rules governs the case. This is of the very essence of judicial duty.

—**John Marshall,** *Marbury v. Madison* (1803)

Courts are the mere instruments of the law, and can will nothing. When they are said to exercise a discretion, it is a mere legal discretion, a discretion to be exercised in discerning the course prescribed by law; and, when that is discerned, it is the duty of the court to follow it. Judicial power is never exercised for the purpose of giving effect to the will of the judge, always for the purpose of giving effect to the will of the legislature; or, in other words, to the will of the law.

—**John Marshall,** *Osborn v. Bank of the United States* (1824)

Stare decisis is usually the wise policy, because in most matters it is more important that the applicable rule of law be settled than that it be settled right. . . . This is commonly true even where the error is a matter of serious concern, provided correction can be had by legislation. But in cases involving the Federal Constitution, where correction through legislative action is practically impossible, this court has often overruled its earlier decisions. The court bows to the lessons of experience and the force of better reasoning, recognizing that the process of trial and error, so fruitful in the physical sciences, is appropriate also in the judicial function.

—**Louis D. Brandeis,** dissenting opinion in
Burnet v. Coronado Oil & Gas Co. (1932)

I took a constitutional oath to obey and to enforce the Constitution of the United States as best I could. I took that just as freely and sincerely as did every senator and every other office holder in the federal government. And obviously, therefore, when there is a conflict between a principle of my faith and the constitutional principle, I have to decide the case as the Constitution requires. That's the oath I took, and that's the oath I follow.

—**William J. Brennan Jr.,** from an interview
with Bill Moyers, May 1987

We are not final because we are infallible, but we are infallible only because we are final.

—**Robert H. Jackson,** concurring
opinion in *Brown v. Allen* (1953)

[T]here is not under our Constitution a judicial remedy for every political mischief, for every undesirable exercise of legislative power. The Framers, carefully and with deliberate forethought, refused so to enthrone the judiciary.

—**Felix Frankfurter,** dissenting
opinion in *Baker v. Carr* (1962)

My years on the Court were crowded with cases involving segregation, voting rights, and other civil rights, malapportionment of representative bodies, incursions on the Bill of Rights, and so forth—all of which had an emotional impact on large segments of the nation. . . . I never took objection to the criticism leveled at me or the Court, and made no attempt to justify publicly any of our decisions. On the other hand, I did want General Eisenhower, who had appointed me to the Court, to know from me that I had not changed my spots; that I was acting from conscience in accordance with my view of the judicial process, even though doing so resulted in unpopularity in some circles.

—**Earl Warren,** in *The Memoirs of
Chief Justice Earl Warren*, 1977

[N]obody knows all the answers when he or she joins the court. You gradually learn about different areas of the law. And you learn through the briefs and arguments of your associates. So it's a continuing learning experience. It's a lot of fun . . . one of the most interesting things anyone can do.

—**John Paul Stevens,** from an interview with Justice
Sandra Day O'Connor, *Newsweek*, December 17, 2010

It is a misfortune if a judge reads his conscious or unconscious sympathy with one side of the other prematurely into the law, and forgets that what seem to him to be first principles are believed by half his fellow men to be wrong.

—**Oliver Wendell Holmes Jr.**, from a speech delivered at Harvard Law School, February 15, 1913

Practicing in the trial work trenches of the law, I saw, too, that when we judges don our robes, it doesn't make us any smarter, but it does serve as a reminder of what's expected of us: Impartiality and independence, collegiality and courage.

—**Neil Gorsuch**, from remarks made during his nomination to the Supreme Court, January 2017

Judges in our system are bound to decide concrete cases, not abstract issues. Each case comes to court based on particular facts and its decision should turn on those facts and the governing law, stated and explained in light of the particular arguments the parties or their representatives present. A judge sworn to decide impartially can offer no forecasts, no hints, for that would show not only disregard for the specifics of the particular case, it would display disdain for the entire judicial process.

—**Ruth Bader Ginsburg**, from the opening statement of her Senate confirmation hearing, Washington, D.C., July 20, 1993

I am one of a small but hardy group of judges and academics in the United States who subscribe to the principle of constitutional interpretation known as originalism. Originalists believe that the provisions of the Constitution have a fixed meaning, which does not change: they mean today what they meant when there were adopted, nothing more and nothing less. That is not to say, of course, that there are not new applications of old constitutional rules.

> —**Antonin Scalia**, in *Scalia Speaks: Reflections on Law, Faith, and Life Well Lived,* edited by Christopher J. Scalia and Edward Whelan, 2017

As for the matter of my judicial philosophy, I didn't have one—and didn't want one. A philosophy that is imposed from without instead of arising organically from day-to-day engagement with the law isn't worth having.

> —**Clarence Thomas**, in *My Grandfather's Son*, 2008

As I see it, the Constitution is primarily a document of majestic specificity, and those specific words have meaning. Absent constitutional amendment, those words continue to bind us as judges, legislators, and executive officials.

> —**Brett Kavanaugh,** from a speech titled "From the Bench: The Constitutional Statesmanship of Chief Justice William Rehnquist," delivered as the AEI 2017 Walter Berns Constitution Day Lecture, September 18, 2017

Courts, however, do not sit or act in a social vacuum. Moral philosophers may debate whether certain inequalities are absolute wrongs, but history makes clear that constitutional principles of equality, like constitutional principles of liberty, property, and due process, evolve over time; what once was a "natural" and "self-evident" ordering later comes to be seen as an artificial and invidious constraint on human potential and freedom. Shifting cultural, political, and social patterns at times come to make past practices appear inconsistent with fundamental principles upon which American society rests. . . .

—**Thurgood Marshall,** concurring in part and dissenting in part in *City of Cleburne v. Cleburne Living Ctr.* (1985)

History or custom or social utility or some compelling sentiment of justice or sometimes perhaps a semi-intuitive apprehension of the pervading spirit of our law, must come to the rescue of the anxious judge, and tell him where to go.

—**Benjamin N. Cardozo,** in *The Nature of the Judicial Process,* 1921

Dissents speak to a future age. It's not simply to say, "My colleagues are wrong and I would do it this way." But the greatest dissents do become court opinions and gradually over time their views become the dominant view. So that's the dissenter's hope: that they are writing not for today, but for tomorrow.

—**Ruth Bader Ginsburg,** from an interview with NPR, May 2002

Merely because a particular activity may not have existed when the Constitution was adopted, or because the framers could not have conceived of a particular method of transacting affairs, cannot mean that general language in the Constitution may not be applied to such a course of conduct. Where the framers of the Constitution have used general language, they have given latitude to those who would later interpret the instrument to make that language applicable to cases that the framers might not have foreseen.

—**William H. Rehnquist**, from "The Notion of a Living Constitution," *Texas Law Review*, May 1976

I have always thought that one of this Court's most important roles is to provide a formidable bulwark against governmental violation of the constitutional safeguards securing in our free society the legitimate expectations of every person to innate human dignity and sense of worth.

—**William J. Brennan Jr.**, dissenting opinion in *Paul v. Davis* (1976)

President Ronald Reagan used to speak of the Soviet constitution. And he noted that it purported to grant wonderful rights of all sorts to people. But those rights were empty promises because that system did not have an independent judiciary to uphold the rule of law and enforce those rights.

—**John G. Roberts Jr.**, from the opening statement of his Senate confirmation hearing, Washington, D.C., September 12, 2005

Justice White always used to say, "When the Court gets a new member, it changes everything." We move the seats around in the courtroom. The seats are by order of seniority, so there will be a shift there, same in the conference room. But more fundamentally, it can cause you to take a fresh look at how things are decided. The new member is going to have a particular view about how issues should be addressed that may be very different from what we've been following for some time. So it's an exciting part of life at the Court.

—**John G. Roberts Jr.,** from an interview with Susan Swain
for C-SPAN, June 19, 2009; quoted from *The Supreme Court: A
C-SPAN Book Featuring the Justices in Their Own Words*, 2010

Power corrupts, and unrestricted power will tempt Supreme Court justices just as history tells us it has tempted other judges. For, unfortunately, judges have not been immune to the seductive influences of power, and given absolute or near absolute power, judges may exercise it to bring about changes that are inimical to freedom and good government.

—**Hugo L. Black,** from a lecture delivered
at Columbia Law School, 1968

We are under a Constitution, but the Constitution is what the judges say it is, and the judiciary is the safeguard of our liberty and of our property under the Constitution.

—**Charles Evans Hughes,** from an address before the
Chamber of Commerce, Elmira, New York, May 3, 1907

Judges are appointed often through the political process. At least there's a political input, but when you put on the robe, at that point the politics is over. And, at that point, a judge must think through each case with the total neutrality that you mentioned. . . All anyone has to ask himself is, Suppose I were on trial? Suppose somebody accused me. Would I want to be judged by whether or not I was popular? Wouldn't I want to be judged on what was true as opposed to what might be popular?

> —**Stephen G. Breyer,** from an interview with
> Bill Moyers for *Frontline* on PBS, 1999

[T]he nature of the profession is that you go on to the next case, and you respect your colleagues. One of the things you learn when you're a judge is that you're not the only person in the room that is objective, disinterested, detached, knowledgeable, unbiased. Your colleagues feel the same way, and you have to recognize that.

> —**Anthony M. Kennedy,** from an interview with Susan Swain
> for C-SPAN, June 25, 2009; quoted in *The Supreme Court: A
> C-SPAN Book Featuring the Justices in Their Own Words*, 2010

We do not have Obama judges or Trump judges, Bush judges or Clinton judges. What we have is an extraordinary group of dedicated judges doing their level best to do equal right to those appearing before them. That independent judiciary is something we should all be thankful for.

> —**John G. Roberts Jr.,** from a statement released
> to the Associated Press, November 21, 2018

As created, the Supreme Court seemed too anemic to endure a long contest for power. . . . Yet in spite of its apparently vulnerable position, this Court has repeatedly overruled and thwarted both the Congress and the Executive. It has been in angry collision with the most dynamic and popular Presidents in our history. Jefferson retaliated with impeachment; Jackson denied its authority; Lincoln disobeyed a writ of the Chief Justice; Theodore Roosevelt, after his Presidency, proposed recall of judicial decisions; Wilson tried to liberalize its membership; and Franklin D. Roosevelt propped to "reorganize it."

> —**Robert H. Jackson,** in *The Struggle for Judicial Supremacy: A Study of a Crisis in American Power Politics,* 1941

I am reminded each day that I render decisions that affect people concretely and that I owe them constant and complete vigilance in checking my assumptions, presumptions and perspectives and ensuring that to the extent that my limited abilities and capabilities permit me, that I reevaluate them and change as circumstances and cases before me requires. I can and do aspire to be greater than the sum total of my experiences but I accept my limitations. I willingly accept that we who judge must not deny the differences resulting from experience and heritage but attempt, as the Supreme Court suggests, continuously to judge when those opinions, sympathies and prejudices are appropriate.

> —**Sonia Sotomayor,** from an address delivered at the "Raising the Bar" symposium, UC Berkeley School of Law, October 26, 2001

The best reason for the public in a democracy to support an independent judiciary with the power of judicial review remains Alexander Hamilton's reason: the public will come to understand the need to occasionally tolerate unpopular Court decisions to help ensure a government that stays within the Constitution's boundaries over time.

—Stephen G. Breyer, in *Making Our Democracy Work: A Judge's View*, 2010

There's a spirit at the Court—and it's not just the justices and their staffs, it just pervades the entire institution—of being proud of the institution you serve, and wanting to give it your best, and make sure that you don't leave it in any worse shape than when you became part of the institution. There's an esprit that is uplifting and energizing. The relationship between the justices is very close, no matter how great our differences. We prize the institution in which we work, and know that it will suffer if we can't get on well with each other.

—Ruth Bader Ginsburg, from an interview at Duke Law School, 2005

The people have seemed to feel that the Supreme Court, whatever its defects, is still the most detached, dispassionate, and trustworthy custodian that our system affords for the translation of abstract into concrete constitutional commands.

—Robert H. Jackson, in *The Supreme Court in the American System of Government*, 1955

[S]ince for 200 years, people have thought in this country that the best guarantee that minorities will not be oppressed, that the Constitution will be lived up to, is to give the very last word to a group of judges who are independent, not because they are wiser— they make mistakes—but because, *by giving them the last word*, there is a better guarantee of that neutrality, insulated from politics, that can help those whom the Constitution wanted to help, that minority [that] might be oppressed.

—**Stephen G. Breyer,** from an interview
with CNN, October 2006

Supreme Court Justices are guardians of the great charter that has served as our Nation's fundamental instrument of government for over 200 years. It is the oldest written constitution still in force in the world. But the Justices do not guard constitutional rights alone; courts share that profound responsibility with Congress, the President, the states, and the people. The constant realization of a more perfect Union, the Constitution's aspiration, requires the widest, broadest, deepest participation on matters of government and government policy.

—**Ruth Bader Ginsburg,** from the opening statement
of her Senate confirmation hearing, July 20, 1993

RACE, GENDER, AND DISCRIMINATION

The experience of Negroes in America has been different in kind, not just in degree, from that of other ethnic groups. It is not merely the history of slavery alone, but also that a whole people were marked as inferior by the law. And that mark has endured.

> —**Thurgood Marshall,** separate opinion in *Regents of the University of California v. Bakke* (1978)

The law knows no finer hour than when it cuts through formal concepts and transitory emotions to protect unpopular citizens against discrimination and persecution.

> —**Frank Murphy,** dissenting opinion in *Falbo v. United States* (1944)

A child born to a Black mother in a state like Mississippi . . . has exactly the same rights as a white baby born to the wealthiest person in the United States. It's not true, but I challenge anyone to say it is not a goal worth working for.

> —**Thurgood Marshall,** from a speech delivered to American Bar Association, 1988

The Constitution voices its disapproval whenever economic discrimination is applied under authority of law against any race, creed or color. A sound democracy cannot allow such discrimination to go unchallenged. Racism is far too virulent today to permit the slightest refusal, in the light of a Constitution that abhors it, to expose and condemn it wherever it appears in the course of a statutory interpretation.

—**Frank Murphy**, concurring opinion in
Steele v. Louisville & N.R. Co. (1944)

I grew up during World War II in a Jewish family. I have memories as a child, even before the war, of being in a car with my parents and passing a place in [Pennsylvania], a resort with a sign out in front that read: "No dogs or Jews allowed." Signs of that kind existed in this country during my childhood. One couldn't help but be sensitive to discrimination living as a Jew in America at the time of World War II.

—**Ruth Bader Ginsburg**, from the opening statement
of her Senate confirmation hearing, July 20, 1993

But in the view of the Constitution, in the eye of the law, there is in this country no superior, dominant, ruling class of citizens. There is no caste here. Our Constitution is color-blind, and neither knows nor tolerates classes among citizens. In respect of civil rights, all citizens are equal before the law. The humblest is the peer of the most powerful.

—**John Marshall Harlan**, from his dissenting
opinion in *Plessy v. Ferguson* (1896)

Korematsu was born on our soil, of parents born in Japan. The Constitution makes him a citizen of the United States by nativity, and a citizen of California by residence. No claim is made that he is not loyal to this country. There is no suggestion that, apart from the matter involved here, he is not law-abiding and well disposed. Korematsu, however, has been convicted of an act not commonly a crime. It consists merely of being present in the state whereof he is a citizen, near the place where he was born, and where all his life he has lived.

>   —**Robert H. Jackson,** dissenting opinion in *Korematsu v. United States* (1944), the infamous decision that upheld the forced relocation of Japanese Americans from western states into War Relocation Centers during World War II

[W]hen racial discrimination herds men into ghettos and makes their ability to buy property turn on the color of their skin, then it too is a relic of slavery.

>   —**Potter Stewart,** *Jones v. Alfred H. Mayer Co.* (1968)

The way to stop discrimination on the basis of race is to speak openly and candidly on the subject of race, and to apply the Constitution with eyes open to the unfortunate effects of centuries of racial discrimination. As members of the judiciary tasked with intervening to carry out the guarantee of equal protection, we ought not sit back and wish away, rather than confront, the racial inequality that exists in our society.

>   —**Sonia Sotomayor,** dissenting opinion in *Schuette v. BAMN* (2014)

I have since deeply regretted the removal order and my own testimony advocating it, because it was not in keeping with our American concept of freedom and the rights of citizens. Whenever I thought of the innocent little children who were torn from home, school friends, and congenial surroundings, I was conscience-stricken. It was wrong to react so impulsively, without positive evidence of disloyalty, even though we felt we had a good motive in the security of our state. It demonstrates the cruelty of war when fear, get-tough military psychology, propaganda, and racial antagonism combine with one's responsibility for public security to produce such acts. I have always believed that I had no prejudice against the Japanese as such except that directly spawned by Pearl Harbor and its aftermath.

—**Earl Warren,** in *The Memoirs of
Chief Justice Earl Warren,* 1977

Nuremberg can remind us that the Holocaust story ended with a fair trial. And that trial, along with the other ways in which law furthers the work of remembrance, can remind us of our eternal aspiration for Justice.

—**Stephen G. Breyer,** from the keynote address delivered
at the Holocaust Memorial Museum during its National
Days of Remembrance, Washington, D.C., May 17, 2011

What is required by Congress is the removal of artificial, arbitrary, and unnecessary barriers to employment when the barriers operate invidiously to discriminate on the basis of racial or other impermissible classification.

—**Warren E. Burger,** *Griggs v. Duke Power Co.* (1971)

[R]ace matters for reasons that really are only skin deep, that cannot be discussed any other way, and that cannot be wished away. Race matters to a young man's view of society when he spends his teenage years watching others tense up as he passes, no matter the neighborhood where he grew up. Race matters to a young woman's sense of self when she states her hometown, and then is pressed, "No, where are you really from?", regardless of how many generations her family has been in the country. Race matters to a young person addressed by a stranger in a foreign language, which he does not understand because only English was spoken at home. Race matters because of the slights, the snickers, the silent judgments that reinforce that most crippling of thoughts: "I do not belong here."

—**Sonia Sotomayor,** dissenting opinion
in *Schuette v. BAMN* (2014)

One wonders whether the majority still believes that race discrimination—or, more accurately, race discrimination against nonwhites—is a problem in our society, or even remembers that it ever was.

—**Harry A. Blackmun,** dissenting opinion in
Ward's Cove Packing Co. v. Atonio (1989)

I would warn any minority student today against the temptations of self-segregation: take support and comfort from your own group as you can, but don't hide within it.

—**Sonia Sotomayor,** in *My Beloved World,* 2013

I yield to no one in my earnest hope that the time will come when an "affirmative action" program is unnecessary and is, in truth, only a relic of the past. I would hope that we could reach this stage within a decade, at the most. But the story of *Brown v. Board of Education*, decided almost a quarter of a century ago, suggests that that hope is a slim one. . . .

—**Harry A. Blackmun,** separate opinion in *Regents of the University of California v. Bakke* (1978)

[T]o know the history of our Nation is to understand its long and lamentable record of stymieing the right of racial minorities to participate in the political process. At first, the majority acted with an open, invidious purpose. Notwithstanding the command of the Fifteenth Amendment, certain States shut racial minorities out of the political process altogether by withholding the right to vote. This Court intervened to preserve that right. The majority tried again, replacing outright bans on voting with literacy tests, good character requirements, poll taxes, and gerrymandering. The Court was not fooled; it invalidated those measures, too. The majority persisted. This time, although it allowed the minority access to the political process, the majority changed the ground rules of the process so as to make it more difficult for the minority, and the minority alone, to obtain policies designed to foster racial integration. Although these political restructurings may not have been discriminatory in purpose, the Court reaffirmed the right of minority members of our society to participate meaningfully and equally in the political process.

—**Sonia Sotomayor,** dissenting opinion in *Schuette v. BAMN* (2014)

I by no means believe that we have yet completed the job of eradicating race as a consideration in the lives of black people. And perhaps of others besides blacks these days, Hispanics and such. And it may take a long while before we get to the day when I can look at you and never see the color of your skin. But I'm convinced that, if there's any place in the world that has a chance of doing that, it's the United States of America.

—**William J. Brennan Jr.**, from an interview
with Bill Moyers, May 1987

One thing has not changed: to doubt the worth of minority students' achievement when they succeed is really only to present another face of the prejudice that would deny them a chance to even try. It is the same prejudice that insists all those destined for success must be cast from the same mold as those who have succeeded before them, a view that experience has already proven a fallacy.

—**Sonia Sotomayor**, in *My Beloved World*, 2013

Once a judicial opinion rationalizes such an order to show that it conforms to the Constitution, or rather rationalizes the Constitution to show that the Constitution sanctions such an order, the Court for all time has validated the principle of racial discrimination in criminal procedure and of transplanting American citizens. The principle then lies about like a loaded weapon, ready for the hand of any authority that can bring forward a plausible claim of an urgent need.

—**Robert H. Jackson**, dissenting opinion
in *Korematsu v. United States* (1944)

The strategy was to go after gender stereotypes, and to erase the law books, in the states and in the nation, of the arbitrary lines that separated the world into two spheres: the world outside the home that belonged to the man, and the world within the home that belonged to the woman.

—**Ruth Bader Ginsburg,** from an interview
at Duke Law School, 2005

Let us not forget that wise men like Oliver Wendell Holmes and Justice Cardozo voted on cases which upheld both sex and race discrimination in our society. Until 1972, no Supreme Court case ever upheld the claim of a woman in a gender discrimination case.

—**Sonia Sotomayor,** from an address delivered
at the "Raising the Bar" symposium, UC
Berkeley School of Law, October 26, 2001

[W]e can only conclude that classifications based upon sex, like classifications based upon race, alienage, or national origin, are inherently suspect, and must therefore be subjected to strict judicial scrutiny.

—**William J. Brennan Jr.**, *Frontiero v. Richardson* (1973)

In order to cultivate a set of leaders with legitimacy in the eyes of the citizenry, it is necessary that the path to leadership be visibly open to talented and qualified individuals of every race and ethnicity.

—**Sandra Day O'Connor,** *Grutter v. Bollinger* (2003)

WOMEN OF THE
SUPREME COURT

My own career in public service was born of necessity. After graduating near the top of my class at Stanford Law School in 1952, I was unable to obtain employment in a private law firm. I did receive one contingent offer of employment—as a legal secretary. But the gender walls that blocked me out of the private sector were more easily hurdled in the public sector, and I first found employment as a deputy county attorney of San Mateo County, California. While I was brought to the position by something short of choice, I came to realize almost immediately what a wonderful path I had taken. . . . Ultimately, these forays into the exciting area of public service led me to the privilege of serving as an assistant attorney general in my state, a state senator, a state judge and a United States Supreme Court Justice. At every step of the way, I felt the thrill of doing something right for a reason that was good. It was the thrill of building bridges.

—**Sandra Day O'Connor,** from a commencement
address presented at Stanford University, June 2004

Women will only have true equality when men share with them the responsibility of bringing up the next generation.

—**Ruth Bader Ginsburg,** from an interview with
ABC News correspondent Lynn Sherr, 2001

My mother told me two things constantly. One was to be a lady, and the other was to be independent. The latter was something very unusual . . . because for most girls growing up in the 1940s, the most important degree was not your B.A., but your "Mrs." "Be a lady" meant don't react to situations with anger, don't consume any of your time with such emotions as envy, because they just sap energy and have no productive value.

—**Ruth Bader Ginsburg,** from an interview
at Duke Law School, 2005

Feminism . . . I think the simplest explanation, and one that captures the idea, is a song that Marlo Thomas sang, "Free to Be You and Me." Free to be, if you were a girl—doctor, lawyer, Indian chief. Anything you want to be. And if you're a boy, and you like teaching, you like nursing, you would like to have a doll, that's OK too. That notion that we should each be free to develop our own talents, whatever they may be, and not be held back by artificial barriers—manmade barriers, certainly not heaven sent.

—**Ruth Bader Ginsburg,** from an interview in
Makers: Women Who Make America, 2012

Sandra Day O'Connor became a Supreme Court Justice as I was preparing to go to law school, and she has served as an inspiration to me ever since. In shattering glass ceiling after glass ceiling, she showed how women could take part as equals in the legal profession.

—**Elena Kagan,** from a statement regarding Sandra
Day O'Connor's public letter announcing her
withdrawal from public life, October 23, 2018

For both men and women the first step in getting power is to become visible to others, and then to put on an impressive show. . . . As women achieve power, the barriers will fall. As society sees what women can do, as women see what women can do, there will be more women out there doing things, and we'll all be better off for it.

> —**Sandra Day O'Connor,** from an address
> delivered at the Sixteenth Annual Olin Conference:
> Women in Power, November 14, 1990

The increasingly full use of the talent of all of this Nation's people holds large promise for the future, but we could not have come to this point—and I surely would not be in this room today—without the determined efforts of men and women who kept dreams of equal citizenship alive in days when few would listen. People like Susan B. Anthony, Elizabeth Cady Stanton, and Harriet Tubman come to mind. I stand on the shoulders of those brave people.

> —**Ruth Bader Ginsburg,** from the opening statement
> of her Senate confirmation hearing, July 20, 1993

I owe a debt of gratitude to two other living Justices. Sandra Day O'Connor and Ruth Bader Ginsburg paved the way for me and so many other women in my generation. Their pioneering lives have created boundless possibilities for women in the law. I thank them for their inspiration and also for the personal kindnesses they have shown me.

> —**Elena Kagan,** from the opening statement of her
> Senate confirmation hearing, June 28, 2010

Most people in poverty in the United States and the world over are women and children, women's earnings here and abroad trail the earnings of men with comparable education and experience, our workplaces do not adequately accommodate the demands of childbearing and child rearing, and we have yet to devise effective ways to ward off sexual harassment at work and domestic violence in our homes. I am optimistic, however, that movement toward enlistment of the talent of all who compose "We, the people," will continue.

—**Ruth Bader Ginsburg**, from the essay
"Ruth Bader Ginsburg's Advice for Living,"
The New York Times, October 1, 2016

How fortunate I feel to be an American and to have been presented with the remarkable opportunities available to the citizens of our country. As a young cowgirl from the Arizona desert, I never could have imagined that one day I would become the first woman justice on the U.S. Supreme Court. I hope that I have inspired young people about civic engagement and helped pave the pathway for women who may have faced obstacles pursuing their careers.

—**Sandra Day O'Connor**, from a letter announcing
her retirement from public life, October 23, 2018

People ask me sometimes, when do you think it will be enough? When will there be enough women on the court? And my answer is when there are nine.

—RUTH BADER GINSBURG, *from remarks made at Georgetown University, February 2015*

Throughout my seventeen years on the bench, I have witnessed the human consequences of my decisions. Those decisions have been made not to serve the interests of any one litigant, but always to serve the larger interest of impartial justice.

—**Sonia Sotomayor**, from the opening statement of her Senate confirmation hearing, July 13, 2009

A question I am often asked: What does women's participation in numbers on the bench add to our judicial system? It is true, as Jeanne Coyne of Minnesota's Supreme Court famously said: at the end of the day, a wise old man and a wise old woman will reach the same decision. But it is also true that women, like persons of different racial groups and ethnic origins, contribute what the late Fifth Circuit Judge Alvin Rubin described as "a distinctive medley of views influenced by differences in biology, cultural impact, and life experience." Our system of justice is surely richer for the diversity of background and experience of its judges. It was poorer when nearly all of its participants were cut from the same mold.

—**Ruth Bader Ginsburg**, from remarks made at an annual meeting of the American Sociological Association, August 11, 2006

RELIGION, MORALITY,
AND CHARACTER

The wise and the good never form the majority of any large society, and it seldom happens that their measures are uniformly adopted. . . . All that the best men can do is, to persevere in doing their duty to their country, and leave the consequences to Him who made it their duty; being neither elated by success, however great, nor discouraged by disappointments however frequent and mortifying.

> —**John Jay**, from a letter to Reverend
> Doctor Price, September 27, 1785

If I have brought any message today, it is this: Have the courage to have your wisdom regarded as stupidity. Be fools for Christ. And have the courage to suffer the contempt of the sophisticated world.

> —**Antonin Scalia**, from a speech delivered at a Living
> the Catholic Faith conference, March 3, 2012

Men may believe what they cannot prove. They may not be put to the proof of their religious doctrines or beliefs. Religious experiences which are as real as life to some may be incomprehensible to others.

> —**William O. Douglas**, *United States v. Ballard* (1944)

I agree with the philosopher who said that money can vanish overnight, power can disappear, reputation can evaporate, but character—personal integrity—is a rock that stays secure.

—STEPHEN G. BREYER, *from a commencement address presented at The New School, May 20, 2005*

I am a judge, born, raised, and proud of being a Jew. The demand for justice, for peace, and for enlightenment runs through the entirety of Jewish history and Jewish tradition. I hope, in all the years I have the good fortune to continue serving on the bench of the Supreme Court of the United States, I will have the strength and courage to remain steadfast in the service of that demand.

—**Ruth Bader Ginsburg**, from remarks made at
the Genesis Foundation Lifetime Achievement
Award ceremony, Tel Aviv, Israel, July 4, 2018

From a profession charged with such responsibilities there must be exacted those qualities of truth-speaking, of a high sense of honor, of granite discretion, of the strictest observance of fiduciary responsibility, that have, throughout the centuries, been compendiously described as "moral character."

—**Felix Frankfurter**, concurring opinion in *Schware v. Board of Bar Examiners of the State of New Mexico* (1957)

There is indeed something deeply wrong with a person who lacks principles, who has no moral core. There are, likewise, certainly values that brook no compromise, and I would count among them integrity, fairness, and the avoidance of cruelty. But I have never accepted the argument that principle is compromised by judging each situation on its own merits, with due appreciation of the idiosyncrasy of human motivation and fallibility.

—**Sonia Sotomayor**, in *My Beloved World*, 2013

Unless you increase, in equal measure with your knowledge, your judgment and character, you will fail in the only thing that is really important, and from which all else follows. You will not be making yourself the best person you can be.

—**Antonin Scalia**, in *Scalia Speaks: Reflections on Law, Faith, and Life Well Lived*, edited by Christopher J. Scalia and Edward Whelan, 2017

Bear in mind that brains and learning, like muscle and physical skill, are articles of commerce. They are bought and sold. You can hire them by the year or by the hour. The only thing in the world not for sale is character.

—**Antonin Scalia**, from a commencement address presented at The College of William & Mary, Williamsburg, Virginia, 1996

FAMILY AND FRIENDSHIP

For sixty years she made life poetry for me and at 88 one must be ready for the end. I shall keep at work and interested while it lasts—though not caring very much for how long.

> —**Oliver Wendell Holmes Jr.**, writing about the passing of his wife, Franny, to Sir Frederick Pollock, 1929

Feeling blessed by what others give to you, recognizing their contributions, and spending time cultivating your relationships with family and friends is critical to finding happiness in life.

> —**Sonia Sotomayor**, from a commencement address presented at New York University, May 16, 2012

My grandmother . . . was also a very strong person. I would talk to her for hours on end, and her life went all the way back to the early days of the Negro, right after Reconstruction. . . . I would just listen to her for hours on end.

> —**Thurgood Marshall**, in *Thurgood Marshall: His Speeches, Writings, Arguments, Opinions, and Reminiscences*, edited by Mark V. Tushnet, 2001

I have a last thank-you. It is to my mother, Celia Amster Bader, the bravest and strongest person I have known, who was taken from me much too soon. . . . I pray that I may be all that she would have been had she lived in an age when women could aspire and achieve and daughters are cherished as much as sons.

—**Ruth Bader Ginsburg,** from a speech
accepting her nomination to the Supreme
Court, Washington, D.C., June 14, 1993

My parents lived the American dream. They grew up in immigrant communities; my mother didn't speak a word of English until she went to school. But she became a legendary teacher and my father a valued lawyer. And they taught me and my two brothers, both high school teachers, that this is the greatest of all countries, because of the freedoms and opportunities it offers its people.

—**Elena Kagan,** from the opening statement of her
Senate confirmation hearing, June 28, 2010

My Latina soul was nourished as I visited and played at my grandmother's house with my cousins and extended family. They were my friends as I grew up. Being a Latina child was watching the adults playing dominos on Saturday night and us kids playing *lotería*, bingo, with my grandmother calling out the numbers which we marked on our cards with chickpeas.

—**Sonia Sotomayor,** from an address delivered
at the "Raising the Bar" symposium, UC
Berkeley School of Law, October 26, 2001

If you have a caring life partner, you help the other person when that person needs it. I had a life partner who thought my work was as important as his, and I think that made all the difference for me.

—**Ruth Bader Ginsburg**, from an interview with Katie Couric for *Yahoo Global News*, July 30, 2014

Justice O'Connor insisted that we have lunch every day when we were sitting. And she insisted, "Now Clarence, you should come to lunch." She was really sweet, but very persistent. I came to lunch, and it was one of the best things I did. It is hard to be angry or bitter at someone and break bread and look them in the eye. . . . It's just nine people, eight people—whoever shows up—having a wonderful lunch together.

—**Clarence Thomas**, from an interview with Susan Swain for C-SPAN, July 29, 2009; quoted in *The Supreme Court: A C-SPAN Book Featuring the Justices in Their Own Words*, 2010

Ruth and I were drawn together, of course, by our similar philosophical proclivities: she was an ardent feminist and a public interest litigator; and I (in the days when I had policy views) opposed affirmative action and thought that standing to litigate should be constricted as narrowly as possible. We have formed a very close friendship, and one of us must be mistaken. Or perhaps both.

—**Antonin Scalia**, in *Scalia Speaks: Reflections on Law, Faith, and Life Well Lived*, edited by Christopher J. Scalia and Edward Whelan, 2017

We went to Wyoming once, where neither of us succeeded in shooting an antelope. We went to Mississippi, where both of us downed a lot of ducks. We took a few daytrips each year to places in Virginia to shoot quail and pheasant. And on the way there and back we talked. He was as funny as he was erudite, as warm as he was brilliant, as charming as he was sharp-witted. We talked about books we were reading. We talked about our two different religions and the meaning of faith. We talked about politics, even though there we usually disagreed. We talked about the love he had for, and the joy he took from, his family. . . . I cherish those conversations with Nino now. I miss him.

—**Elena Kagan**, in "In Memoriam: Justice Antonin Scalia," *Harvard Law Review*, April 2019

There's no sadder day around here than when a member of this Court leaves. When Justice Souter announced that he was leaving— remember, I've served almost eighteen years with him. He becomes your friend. You don't have to agree, but he's your friend. When you hear one of your colleagues is sick, it's one of your family members who's sick.

—**Clarence Thomas**, from an interview with Susan Swain for C-SPAN, July 29, 2009; quoted in *The Supreme Court: A C-SPAN Book Featuring the Justices in Their Own Words*, 2010

Well, my best friend was my dear spouse. Marty was always my best friend.

—**Ruth Bader Ginsburg**, from an interview on *The Rachel Maddow Show*, February 17, 2015

Potter Stewart had a very strong feeling for the Court as an institution, and for the way that the Court ought to work. He realized that if all nine justices simply buried themselves in their chambers working only according to their own schedules, without responding to circulations from their colleagues, long and unnecessary delays could ensue. . . . He was also, I think, of all the colleagues with whom I have served, the one least influenced by considerations extraneous to the strictly legal aspects of a case—he was, that is, the quintessential judge.

—**William H. Rehnquist,** in *The Supreme Court,* 1987

Although occasionally a stern figure on the bench, the Chief had a whimsical side. He was a great one for games—tennis, croquet, bridge, poker, and board games were favorites. I have never witnessed a more enthusiastic charades player. . . . There will be time enough to assess and debate his impact on the law. For those of us fortunate enough to have known him, however, he will always be remembered first and foremost as a genuinely kind, thoughtful, and decent man.

—**John G. Roberts Jr.,** in "In Memoriam: William H. Rehnquist," *Harvard Law Review,* November 2005

I've had 111 law clerks. . . . It's like having this marvelous family, and they're married and they have children, so I feel like a grandparent of one thousand children. It's really nice.

—**Stephen G. Breyer,** interview with Brian Lamb for C-SPAN, June 17, 2009; quoted in *The Supreme Court: A C-SPAN Book Featuring the Justices in Their Own Words,* 2010

But our friend Bill Brennan is gone from us. His leave taking was exact in time and place, and to our friend we do have to say a farewell. The hard thing is not just to speak the words but to speak words that can do justice to friendship as immoderate and as prodigal as Bill Brennan's friendship was. He made us members of a huge family by adoption, and when we were with him every one of us always felt like the favorite child.

> —**David H. Souter**, from remarks made at the funeral
> mass for Justice William J. Brennan Jr., July 29, 1997

Most of all, I prized the rare talent Justice Scalia possessed for making even the most sober judge smile. When we sat side by side on the D.C. Circuit, I occasionally pinched myself hard to avoid uncontrollable laughter in response to one of his quips. On the Supreme Court, where we were separated by a few seats, notes he sent my way elicited a similar reaction.

> —**Ruth Bader Ginsburg**, from the foreword to *Scalia
> Speaks: Reflections on Law, Faith, and Life Well Lived,*
> edited by Christopher J. Scalia and Edward Whelan, 2017

He was, indeed, a magnificent performer. How blessed I was to have a working colleague and dear friend of such captivating brilliance, high spirits, and quick wit. In the words of a duet for tenor Scalia and soprano Ginsburg, we were different, yes, in our interpretation of written texts, yet one in our reverence for the Court and its place in the U.S. system of governance.

> —**Ruth Bader Ginsburg**, from her eulogy for Justice
> Antonin Scalia, Washington, D.C., March 1, 2016

JUDICIAL WIT

The acme of judicial distinction means the ability to look a lawyer straight in the eyes for two hours and not to hear a damned word he says.

—**John Marshall**, in "John Marshall's
Living Legacy," *Life*, August 29, 1955

I do not suppose that civilization will come to an end whichever way this case is decided.

—**Oliver Wendell Holmes Jr.**, dissenting
opinion in *Haddock v. Haddock* (1906)

I have vivid memories of the first judicial handshake I experienced. That was mostly due to Justice Byron White, an NFL football star who possessed, as I soon learned the hard way, a viselike grip. As I shook each of my new colleagues' hands, Justice Byron White shook my hand in his with such force that I felt tears spring to my eyes from the pain! From then on, I resolved to grab his thumb instead of giving him my hand. That was a preemptive measure I knew I needed to take to endure the many handshakes to come in the years ahead!

—**Sandra Day O'Connor**, in *Out of Order: Stories
from the History of the Supreme Court*, 2013

I always turn to the sports section first. The sports page records people's accomplishments; the front page nothing but man's failures.

> —**Earl Warren**, in "Scorecard," *Sports Illustrated*, July 21, 1968

Some people are inherently likeable. If you're not—work on it. It may even improve your social life.

> —**Antonin Scalia**, *Making Your Case: The Art of Persuading Judges*, by Antonin Scalia and Bryan A. Garner, 2008

I find the workload of what I do sufficiently great that when the term of court starts I undergo a sort of annual intellectual lobotomy.

> —**David H. Souter**, as quoted in *The New York Times*, May 7, 2009

While some of the tales of woe emanating from the court are enough to bring tears to the eyes, it is true that only Supreme Court justices and schoolchildren are expected to and do take the entire summer off.

> —**John G. Roberts Jr.**, from remarks made while working as a young lawyer in the Reagan White House, 1983

I have a lifetime appointment and I intend to serve it. I expect to die at 110, shot by a jealous husband.

—THURGOOD MARSHALL, *from remarks made to the* International Herald Tribune, *January 15, 1990*

Among my favorite Scalia stories—when President Clinton was mulling over his first nomination to the Supreme Court, Justice Scalia was asked: "If you were stranded on a desert island with your new Court colleague, who would you prefer, Larry Tribe or Mario Cuomo?" Scalia answered quickly and distinctly: "Ruth Bader Ginsburg." And within days, the President chose me.

—**Ruth Bader Ginsburg**, from her eulogy for Justice Antonin Scalia, Washington, D.C., March 1, 2016

I used to say that, as Solicitor General, I made three arguments of every case. First came the one that I planned—as I thought, logical, coherent, complete. Second was the one actually presented— interrupted, incoherent, disjointed, disappointing. The third was the utterly devastating argument that I thought of after going to bed that night.

—**Robert H. Jackson**, in "Advocacy Before the United States Supreme Court," *Cornell Law Review*, 1951

WISDOM OF THE JUSTICES

[W]e pause to become conscious of our national life and to rejoice in it, to recall what our country has done for each of us, and to ask ourselves what we can do for the country in return.

> —**Oliver Wendell Holmes Jr.**, from a Memorial Day address delivered before the John Sedgwick Post No. 4, Grand Army of the Republic veterans' organization, New Hampshire, May 30, 1884

Whether acting in the legal, governmental, or private realm, one concerned and dedicated person can meaningfully affect what some consider an uncaring world. So give freely of yourself always to your family, your friends, your community, and your country. The world will pay you back many times over.

> —**Sandra Day O'Connor,** in *The Majesty of the Law: Reflections of a Supreme Court Justice,* 2003

What the lawyer needs to redeem himself is not more ability . . . but the moral courage in the face of financial loss and personal ill-will to stand for right and justice.

> —**Louis D. Brandeis,** from a speech delivered to the Harvard Law Review Association, June 22, 1907

So often in life, things that you regard as an impediment turn out to be great, good fortune.

—RUTH BADER GINSBURG, from an interview in *Makers: Women Who Make America*, 2012

[I]f we focus our energies on sharing ideas, finding solutions and using what is right with America to remedy what is wrong with it, we can make a difference. Our nation needs bridges, and bridges are built by those who look to the future and dedicate themselves to helping others.

—**Sandra Day O'Connor,** from a commencement address presented at Stanford University, June 13, 2004

I've led a school whose faculty and students examine and discuss and debate every aspect of our law and legal system. And what I've learned most is that no one has a monopoly on truth or wisdom. I've learned that we make progress by listening to each other, across every apparent political or ideological divide.

—**Elena Kagan,** from the opening statement of her Senate confirmation hearing, June 28, 2010

And as you pursue your paths in life, leave tracks. Just as others have been way pavers for you, so you should aid those who will follow in your way. Do your part to help move society to the place you would like it to be for the health and well-being of generations following your own.

—**Ruth Bader Ginsburg,** from a commencement address presented at Brown University, May 26, 2002

It is not easy to detest an extremist philosophy and yet insist on the right of a man to advocate it freely. Yet, apparently we must do just this if we are to practice our faith in democracy. . . . We must never forget that the democratic way is not to crush the alien view but to let it be heard and to defeat it by demonstrating that our way of living contributes the most to human happiness.

—**Frank Murphy**, from a speech titled "Civil Liberties," delivered over N.B.C., March 27, 1939

[O]ur Nation's commitment to basic principles of democracy, liberty, and fairness has depended upon a tradition of commitment to the enterprise, built gradually over time, not just by politicians or by judges, but by millions of ordinary citizens. My parents' generation passed that tradition on to mine; we must to yours; and you must to your children's. Otherwise, our society, and our law—however decent and fair in principle—will not work in practice.

—**Stephen G. Breyer**, from a commencement address presented at The New School, May 20, 2005

QUOTES ABOUT THE
SUPREME COURT JUSTICES

In nominating you for the important Station, which you now fill, I
not only acted in conformity to my best judgment but I trust I did a
grateful thing to the good citizens of these United States; and I have
a full confidence that the love which you bear to our country, and a
desire to promote the general happiness, will not suffer you to hesitate
a moment to bring into action the talents, knowledge and integrity
which are so necessary to be exercised at the head of that department
which must be considered the keystone of our political fabric.

> —George Washington, from a letter to John Jay
> commissioning Jay to the Supreme Court,
> October 5, 1789

[T]here fell to Marshall perhaps the greatest place that ever was
filled by a judge; but when I consider his might, his justice, and
his wisdom, I do fully believe that if American law were to be
represented by a single figure, sceptic and worshipper alike would
agree without dispute that the figure could be one alone, and that one,
John Marshall.

> —Oliver Wendell Holmes Jr., from an answer to a
> motion that the Court adjourn on February 4, 1901,
> for the 100th anniversary of the day on which
> John Marshall took his seat as Chief Justice

[William H.] Taft is the only person ever to serve as both President of the United States and Chief Justice, and his experience as President served him well on the Court. When he was appointed Chief Justice in 1921, the Court had fallen nearly five years behind in its docket. He resolved this caseload congestion in the Court by convincing Congress to pass the Judiciary Act of 1925—also known as the Certiorari Act—which gave the Court discretion as to which cases to hear. Some members of Congress were doubtful—why shouldn't every litigant have a right to get a decision on his case from the Supreme Court? Taft responded that in each case, there had already been one trial and one appeal. "Two courts are enough for justice," he said. To obtain still a third hearing in the Supreme Court, there should be some question involved more important than just who wins this lawsuit. . . . But perhaps Chief Justice Taft's most lasting contribution to the Supreme Court of the United States was in convincing Congress to give the Court a building of its own.

—**William H. Rehnquist**, remarks made
during the dedication of the Ohio Judicial
Center, Columbus, Ohio, May 15, 2004

Your long practical experience and intimate knowledge of affairs, the wide range of your researches and your grasp of the most difficult problems, together with your power of analysis and your thoroughness in exposition, have made your judicial career one of extraordinary distinction and far-reaching influence.

—from a farewell letter to **Louis D. Brandeis** from his
fellow Supreme Court Justices upon his retirement, 1939

No appointee to the Court before or since has combined the scholarly and intellectual credentials possessed by the diminutive professor. Nor was he by any stretch of the imagination a recluse or wallflower; he radiated charm and made great efforts to persuade others to his views. And yet, though he served on the Court for more than twenty years, his influence fell far short of what had been expected. He sought to make disciples of his colleagues, not realizing that their commissions, if not their intellects or knowledge, made them his equals on the Court. He never fully made the transition from the professor's lectern—where he could expound his views endlessly—to a collegial body where long-term success depended on winning over others of quite different backgrounds.

> —**William H. Rehnquist**, recalling **Justice**
> **Felix Frankfurter**, in *The Supreme Court*
> by William H. Rehnquist, 1987

He was, in short, a lawyer's lawyer with a conscience—a believer in hard and careful work and the value of lawyering. . . . When Frankfurter retired, Harlan became the standard bearer of judicial restraint, federalism, and deference to legislatures, but he shared with his grandfather a concern for civil rights, especially those of African Americans, and free speech.

> —about **John Marshall Harlan II**, the grandson
> of John Marshall Harlan, in *The Supreme Court:*
> *An Essential History* by Peter Charles Hoffer,
> Williamjames Hull Hoffer, and N.E.H Hull, 2007

My gift of John Marshall to the people of the United States was the proudest act of my life.

—**John Adams, 1825**

"[T]he biggest damn fool mistake I ever made."

— **Earl Warren,** paraphrasing **President Eisenhower** in reference to his appointment of Warren to the Supreme Court

[Earl] Warren . . . recognized that America's formative pathology—its racism—was a terminal cancer that must be dealt with urgently. He engineered the boldest stroke against segregation since Reconstruction.

—**Michael O'Donnell,** in "Commander v. Chief," *The Atlantic*, April 2018

As a result of his career as a lawyer and as a judge, Thurgood Marshall left an indelible mark, not just upon the law, but upon his country. Inscribed above the front entrance to the Supreme Court building are the words "Equal justice under law." Surely no one individual did more to make these words a reality than Thurgood Marshall.

—**William H. Rehnquist,** from remarks made at **Thurgood Marshall's** Memorial Service, Washington, D.C., January 1993

[M]y dear, dear colleague and very close friend Hugo Black had a view on constitutional interpretation that has not prevailed. And I suggest that the more prevailing view is one that I share, that its broad principles have to be interpreted in the context of the day and of the problems of the time. And not in the context of what was the case in 1791.

> —**William J. Brennan Jr.**, from an interview
> with Bill Moyers, May 1987

Justice Brennan was a remarkable person. Part of what made him so extraordinary was that he was filled with joy. He always had a sparkle in his eye, a kind word, and a hand on your arm when he spoke with you. . . . Brennan was a very hard worker. He came into the office every morning before 7:30, so he could review all of the work his law clerks had left him late the night before. He met with the clerks every morning for coffee for an hour, during which time we discussed the cases on the docket, drafts of opinions we had written, or cert petitions he'd reviewed by himself. He was the only Justice who read all the cert petitions himself. We also talked about the Vietnam War, Watergate, and the Washington Redskins. Brennan was a real person. He was smart, kindhearted, thoughtful, and exuberant.

> —**Geoffrey R. Stone,** in "Honoring the Legacies
> of Justices William J. Brennan Jr., and Justice
> Thurgood Marshall," *Indiana Law Review*, 2010

Justice Powell's non-ideological conservatism reflected his own innate courtesy and grace. It was tempered by, indeed based upon, habits of empathy and compassion that were immensely appealing. . . . [C]ollege, law school, military service, and lawyer's work—taught him the importance of close personal bonds, community involvement, taking responsibility, a sense of belonging to a place. He had a vivid sense of the personal rewards, as well as the costs, of public service, and he thought it absolutely critical that institutions that afforded the opportunity for service be nurtured and preserved.

—**Christina B. Whitman**, in "In Memoriam: Lewis F. Powell Jr.," *Harvard Law Review*, 1999

Let me begin by expressing my admiration for the work performed by Justice Elena Kagan, who now occupies the seat on the Supreme Court that became vacant when I retired a few years ago. She has written opinion after opinion, both for the Court and in dissent, which expresses my reaction to a particular issue that is far more articulate and persuasive than anything I might have written. The fact that she is performing so capably is particularly gratifying because it confirms my judgment that my retirement would benefit the public as well as myself. Thanks to Elena, I have never regretted my decision to retire.

—**John Paul Stevens**, from remarks made at a University of Miami Law Review symposium, February 7, 2015

Sandra Day O'Connor's voice has done enormous good in the pursuit of justice for all in our land and world. She has done more to promote collegiality among the Court's members, and with our counterparts abroad, than any other Justice, past or present. In her work and days, she strived mightily to make what was momentous for women in 1981, the year she was appointed to the Court, no longer extraordinary, but entirely expectable. In that effort, I am among legions of women endeavoring to follow her lead.

> —**Ruth Bader Ginsburg,** from a statement regarding
> **Justice O'Connor's** public letter announcing her
> withdrawal from public life, October 23, 2018

I miss your warmth, your sense of humor, that Western touch, and of course your legal mind. You, my friend, will take your place in history, not just as the first woman appointed to the Supreme Court, but also as one of its greatest Justices.

> —**Stephen G. Breyer,** from a statement regarding
> **Justice O'Connor's** public letter announcing her
> withdrawal from public life, October 23, 2018

His integrity, humility, and independence, his deep devotion to the Court, and his profound commitment to the rule of law—all these qualities are models for everyone who wears, or hopes to wear, a judge's robe.

> —**Elena Kagan,** referring to **Justice John Paul
> Stevens** during the opening statement of her
> Senate confirmation hearing, June 28, 2010

CONTRIBUTORS

Samuel A. Alito Jr. *(b. 1950)* — Appointed by George W. Bush as an associate justice in 2006, he became one of the most conservative justices on the Court. Notably, he wrote the majority opinion in the highly contentious *Burwell v. Hobby Lobby Stores,* in which the Court ruled that a closely held for-profit corporation could not be compelled to provide birth control to employees under its health care plans. According to the Court, the mandate violated the Free Exercise Clause of the First Amendment.

Hugo L. Black *(1886–1971)* — Born and raised in the South, he infamously belonged to the KKK for two years in the 1920s, though he strongly denounced his prior membership shortly after being confirmed to the Court. Appointed by President Franklin D. Roosevelt as an associate justice in 1937, he was a staunch supporter of the New Deal and was well known for his strict reading of the Constitution and for his literal reading of the First Amendment. After serving on the Court for 34 years, he suffered a stroke in 1971, retired, and died one week later.

Harry A. Blackmun *(1908–1999)* — A childhood friend of Warren E. Burger, he was appointed to the Court as an associate justice by President Richard M. Nixon in 1970. A pragmatic jurist, he was concerned with the impact the Court's decisions would have upon people in their daily lives. He is best known for writing the majority opinion in *Roe v. Wade* in 1973. Though he faced harsh criticism and even received death threats as a result of the opinion, he continued to champion abortion rights and privacy rights for the rest of his career. By the time he retired in 1990, he had evolved into a staunch protector of civil liberties and individual rights.

Louis D. Brandeis *(1856–1941)* — Known as "The People's Lawyer" for his advocacy of public interest cases and for his pro bono work, he was appointed by President Woodrow Wilson as an associate justice in 1916. A staunch supporter of civil liberties, individual rights, and First Amendment rights, he authored hundreds of carefully crafted opinions, with many of his dissenting opinions later becoming law. His famous dissenting opinion in *Olmstead v. United States* laid the framework for the constitutional right to privacy. A towering presence throughout his legal career, he retired from the Court in 1939 at the age of 83.

William J. Brennan Jr. *(1906–1997)* — Appointed as an associate justice by President Dwight D. Eisenhower in 1956, he was a champion of civil rights, civil liberties, and individual rights. He wrote more than 1,300 opinions during his 34 years on the Court, including the majority opinion in *Baker v. Carr*, which set forth the "one person, one vote" principle, and in *Frontiero v. Richardson,* which ruled that gender discrimination was a violation of the Equal Protection Clause. A fierce opponent of the death penalty and supporter of abortion rights, he retired from the Court in 1990 and was awarded the Presidential Medal of Freedom by President Bill Clinton in 1993.

Stephen G. Breyer *(b. 1938)* — An influential professor and a respected jurist, he was appointed by President Bill Clinton as an associate justice in 1994. He is a pragmatic jurist who rejects the rigid interpretation of the Constitution favored by the Court's strict constructionists. Rather, he favors considering the real-life consequences of the Court's decisions and is among the justices who view the Constitution as a "living" document that needs nuanced interpretation.

Warren E. Burger *(1907–1995)* — Appointed by President Richard M. Nixon as chief justice in 1969, he was a conservative voice on the Court in some areas, particularly when it came to the rights of the accused. But he notably joined with the liberal justices for such landmark cases as *Reed v. Reed*, in which gender discrimination was ruled unconstitutional, and in *Roe v. Wade*, in which access to legal abortion was affirmed. He retired in 1986 as the longest-serving chief justice of the twentieth century, and was awarded the Presidential Medal of Freedom by President Ronald Reagan in 1988.

Benjamin N. Cardozo *(1870–1938)* — A legal scholar and highly esteemed jurist on the New York Court of Appeals, he was appointed by President Herbert Hoover as an associate justice in 1932. Generally joining the liberals on the Court, he was often in dissent, as the conservative majority consistently opposed FDR's New Deal legislation. He is famously known for his opinion in *Palko v. Connecticut*, in which he articulated the standard for determining which provisions of the Bill of Rights would be applicable to the states—a standard that would guide the Court until 1969. Only six years into his tenure on the Court, he suffered a series of heart attacks and died of a stroke in July of 1938.

Tom C. Clark *(1899–1977)* — Appointed in 1949 by President Harry S. Truman, he was a moderate voice on the Court, but he was also the author of several majority opinions in important civil liberties cases. He is perhaps best known for writing the opinion of the Court in *Mapp v. Ohio*, which held that evidence seized illegally could not be used against a defendant in state court. He resigned from the Court in 1967 after his son, William Ramsey Clark, was nominated by President Johnson to be the attorney general.

William O. Douglas *(1898–1980)* — Appointed by President Franklin D. Roosevelt, he is the longest-serving justice in the history of the Court, having sat on the bench from 1939 until 1975. A staunch defender of civil liberties and First Amendment rights, he was known as a maverick, both on the Court and in his personal life, as well as a tireless advocate for the environment.

Abe Fortas *(1910–1982)* — Appointed by President Lyndon B. Johnson as an associate justice in 1965, he is known for his cases in the area of juvenile justice. He authored opinions in such landmark cases as *In re Gault*, which extended constitutional protections to juveniles in criminal proceedings, and *Tinker v. Des Moines*, which ruled that students had a constitutional right to protest the Vietnam War by wearing black armbands. His career on the Supreme Court was cut short when he was forced to resign in 1969 amid allegations of financial improprieties. He continued to practice law until his death in 1982.

Felix Frankfurter *(1882–1965)* — Born in Vienna, he emigrated to New York with his family when he was twelve and went on to graduate first in his class from Harvard Law School. A brilliant professor of law at Harvard, and a friend and advisor to President Franklin D. Roosevelt, he was appointed to the Court as an associate justice in 1939. His strict belief in the philosophy of judicial restraint was his guiding principle during his tenure on the Court and left him sternly in dissent for many of the landmark decisions of the Warren Court. Retiring in 1962, he was awarded the Presidential Medal of Freedom by President John F. Kennedy in 1963.

Ruth Bader Ginsburg *(b. 1933)* — A professor and ground-breaking litigator for gender equality in her legal career prior to joining the Court, she was appointed by President Bill Clinton as an associate justice in 1993 and became the second woman to sit on the Court. She is a prudent jurist who carefully builds on precedent and is a strong voice for civil rights and gender equality. She wrote for the Court in the landmark case of *United States v. Virginia*, which struck down the male-only admissions policy of the Virginia Military Institute as unconstitutional. Known as a feminist icon and leader, she was named one of the 100 Most Powerful Women in 2009 by *Forbes* and one of the World's Greatest Leaders in 2016 by *Fortune*.

Arthur J. Goldberg *(1908–1990)* — Appointed by President John F. Kennedy as an associate justice in 1962, he championed civil rights, civil liberties, and the right to privacy. His tenure on the Court was brief, however, as he resigned to become the U.S. Ambassador to the United Nations in 1965. He resigned from this position in 1968 after growing increasingly frustrated with the Vietnam War, eventually returning to the private practice of law. He was awarded the Presidential Medal of Freedom in 1978 by President Jimmy Carter.

Neil Gorsuch *(b. 1967)* — Appointed by President Donald J. Trump as an associate justice in 2017, he is a conservative voice on the Court and an originalist in his interpretation of the Constitution. He is a strong proponent of states' rights, and he has taken an expansive view in the area of religious liberty.

John Marshall Harlan *(1833–1911)* — Appointed by President Rutherford B. Hayes in 1877, he served as an associate justice for close to 34 years. He evolved into a staunch supporter of civil rights despite being born into a slaveholding family and owning slaves himself until the ratification of the Thirteenth Amendment. In 1896, he was famously the sole dissenter in *Plessy* *v. Ferguson*, in which the majority upheld the state's right to engage in systematic racial segregation. He served on the Court from 1877 until his death in 1911.

John Marshall Harlan II *(1899–1971)* — The grandson of Supreme Court Justice John Marshall Harlan, he was appointed by President Dwight D. Eisenhower as an associate justice in 1955. He was in the majority for several landmark civil rights and civil liberty cases during his tenure, including *Loving v. Virginia* and *Griswold v. Connecticut,* wherein the Court ruled that a ban on contraceptives was a violation of a married couple's right to privacy. Facing serious illness, he retired from the Court in 1971 and died several months later.

Oliver Wendell Holmes Jr. *(1841–1935)* — Appointed by President Theodore Roosevelt as an associate justice in 1902, he wrote more than 870 opinions while on the Court. He was known as "The Great Dissenter" for his eloquent dissenting opinions, many of which became law in later years. He famously wrote for the Court in *Schenck v. United States*, which set forth the "clear and present danger" standard for the regulation of free speech, and he continued to champion an expansive view of the First Amendment throughout his 30-year career on the Court. He retired at the age of 90.

Charles Evans Hughes *(1862–1948)* — Appointed by President William H. Taft as an associate justice, he served from 1910 to 1916, resigning when he received the Republican presidential nomination. He later served as Secretary of State and was again appointed to the Supreme Court in 1930, this time as chief justice, by President Herbert Hoover. Hughes led the Court during the great tumult surrounding FDR's New Deal, striking down key pieces of New Deal legislation and prompting FDR's failed attempt to "pack the Court" with additional justices. Ultimately, Hughes began leading the Court in a more pro–New Deal direction. He retired in 1941, at nearly 80 years old.

Robert H. Jackson *(1892–1954)* — Appointed by President Franklin D. Roosevelt as an associate justice in 1941, he was an advocate of judicial restraint and a strong supporter of civil liberties. He wrote for the Court in *West Virginia Board of Education v. Barnette*, which ruled that schoolchildren had a constitutional right to refuse to recite the Pledge of Allegiance. He famously dissented in the *Korematsu* case, arguing against the country's intern-ment of Japanese Americans during World War II. In 1945, he took leave from the Court to serve as Chief U.S. Prosecutor in the Nuremberg Trials, returning to the bench thereafter until his death in 1954, at the age of 62.

John Jay *(1745–1829)* — Appointed by President George Washington, he was the first chief justice of the Supreme Court. He served from 1789 to 1795, at which time he resigned from the Court to serve as the governor of New York. After six years as governor, he retired from public service and enjoyed a productive retirement for close to 30 years.

Elena Kagan *(b. 1960)* — An influential professor and advisor to President Bill Clinton, she was appointed by President Barack Obama as an associ-ate justice in 2010. Known for her sharp intellect and her ability to build consensus, she is aligned with the liberal members of the Court. She was in the majority for the landmark case *Obergefell v. Hodges*, which ruled in favor of same-sex marriage. A strict believer in the separation of church and state, she wrote a powerful dissent in *Town of Greece v. Galloway* about the divisive effects of using Christian prayers at public meetings.

Brett Kavanaugh *(b. 1965)* — Appointed by President Donald J. Trump as an associate justice in 2018, he faced a highly contentious confirmation hearing when allegations of a sexual assault from the 1980s surfaced. He adamantly denied the allegations and was narrowly confirmed by the Senate. His tenure on the Court began on October 9, 2018; he favors a pragmatic approach and has indicated a strong belief in the rule of precedent.

Anthony M. Kennedy *(b. 1936)* — Appointed by President Ronald Reagan as an associate justice in 1988, he was a key moderate voice on the Court and an important "swing vote" between the liberal and conservative justices. A strong supporter of individual rights, he was the deciding vote in the contentious *Planned Parenthood v. Casey*, which reaffirmed the holding in *Roe v. Wade*. Likewise, he has championed gay and lesbian rights, culminating in his decision in *Obergefell*, which ruled that same-sex marriage was a constitutional right. He retired in July 2018.

John Marshall *(1755–1835)* — Considered the most influential justice in the history of the Court, he was appointed by President John Adams as chief justice in 1801 and served until 1835. He was responsible for elevating the Court to a co-equal branch of government alongside the executive and legislative branches, and he helped establish it as the ultimate arbiter in interpreting the Constitution. He delivered more than 1,000 decisions and authored more than 500 opinions during his 34 masterful years on the Court.

Thurgood Marshall *(1908–1993)* — Born the great-grandchild of slaves, he was an unsurpassed litigator in the civil rights movement. He argued an historic number of cases before the Court, including the seminal *Brown v. Board of Education*, which ended racial segregation in public schools. He was appointed by President Lyndon B. Johnson as an associate justice in 1967, becoming the first African American to sit on the Supreme Court, where he continued to be an unwavering supporter of civil rights, civil liberties, and privacy rights. He retired in 1991 at the age of 82, and was posthumously awarded the Presidential Medal of Freedom in 1993.

Frank Murphy *(1890–1949)* — Appointed by President Franklin D. Roosevelt, he served as an associate justice for close to ten years. Though he faced criticism for being a results-oriented jurist, he was known as a staunch defender of civil liberties. His most famous dissent was in *Korematsu v. United States*, in which he called the government's internment of Japanese Americans living on the West Coast during World War II the "legalization of racism." He served on the Court from 1940 to his untimely death in 1949.

Sandra Day O'Connor *(b. 1930)* — Appointed by President Ronald Reagan as an associate justice in 1981, she became the first woman to sit on the Supreme Court. A practical jurist and a moderate conservative on the Court, she was an independent voter and an important swing vote in many contentious cases. Notably, she voted in *Planned Parenthood v. Casey* to uphold the central holding of *Roe v. Wade*. Known for her sharp intellect and negotiation skills, she retired in 2006 and was awarded the Presidential Medal of Freedom in 2009. In 2018, she stepped away from public life after revealing that she'd been diagnosed with dementia.

Lewis F. Powell Jr. *(1907–1998)* — Appointed by President Richard M. Nixon as an associate justice in 1972, he was a pragmatic jurist and moderate voice on the Court. While conservative in criminal justice matters, he notably sided with the liberal justices in landmark decisions such as *Roe v. Wade* and wrote the opinion of the Court in the famous *Regents of the University of California v. Bakke* case, which ruled that affirmative action was constitutional as a means of achieving diversity. He retired from the Court in 1987.

William H. Rehnquist *(1924–2005)* — Appointed by President Richard M. Nixon as an associate justice in 1972, he was appointed chief justice by President Ronald Reagan in 1986. A staunch conservative, he favored a narrow reading of the Constitution that emphasized states' rights. His notable cases include *United States v. Lopez*, which held that Congress had exceeded its power under the Commerce Clause in criminalizing the possession of guns in school zones. Considered a fair and efficient chief justice, he remained on the Court until his death in 2005.

John G. Roberts Jr. *(b. 1955)* — Appointed by George W. Bush as chief justice in 2005, he became the youngest chief justice to sit on the Court since John Marshall. Despite his overall conservative judicial philosophy, he has shown a willingness to join with the liberal members of the Court. Whereas he opposed the majority's legalization of gay marriage in *Obergefell*, he sided with the liberal justices to uphold the Affordable Care Act on two occasions. He has been described as a fair and effective chief justice by his fellow justices and an excellent spokesperson for the Court.

Wiley B. Rutledge *(1894–1949)* — Appointed by President Franklin D. Roosevelt as an associate justice in 1943, he was a strong liberal voice on the Court and a consistent supporter of civil rights, civil liberties, and First Amendment rights. He famously dissented in *In re Yamashita* in 1946, urging the Court to apply the fundamental rules of fairness for proceedings involving war criminals. After six years on the Court, he died suddenly of a stroke at only 55 years old.

Antonin Scalia *(1936–2016)* — Appointed by President Ronald Reagan in 1986 as an associate justice, he became the first Italian American justice on the Court. He was a staunch originalist in his judicial philosophy, seeking to follow the original meaning of the Constitution as intended by the Framers. He was known to write scathing rebukes of his fellow justices in dissent. His notable cases include *District of Columbia v. Heller*, in which the Court ruled that the Second Amendment protects an individual's right to bear arms for lawful use. In 2018, he was posthumously awarded the Presidential Medal of Freedom by President Donald J. Trump. ·

Sonia Sotomayor *(b. 1954)* — Appointed by President Barack Obama as an associate justice in 2009, she became the third woman and first Hispanic and Latina justice on the Court. She is a strong voice for individual rights, race and gender equality, and for the rights of the accused and imprisoned. She joined with the majority in the landmark case *Obergefell v Hodges*, which ruled in favor of same-sex marriage. In *Schuette v. Coalition to Defend Affirmative Action*, she wrote a powerful dissent and offered a frank analysis of the impact of race and racism in America.

David H. Souter *(b. 1939)* — Appointed by President George H. W. Bush in 1990 as an associate justice, he began his tenure more closely aligned with the conservative members of the Court. In his later years on the bench, he gravitated more toward his liberal colleagues. He notably joined in the plurality in *Planned Parenthood v. Casey*, which reaffirmed the Court's decision in *Roe v. Wade*. Likewise, he defended affirmative action, campaign finance restrictions, and the strict separation of church and state. Retiring from the Court in 2009, he continues to hear cases by designation at the circuit court level.

John Paul Stevens *(b. 1920)* — Appointed by President Gerald R. Ford as an associate justice in 1975, he was a fiercely independent voice on the Court, though eventually became more closely aligned with its liberal members. He wrote the opinion of the Court in *Wallace v. Jaffree*, which ruled that a minute of silence for meditation or silent prayer in public school violated the Establishment Clause. He penned a powerful dissent in *Bush v. Gore*, the ruling that awarded the presidency to George W. Bush. He retired in 2010 at the age of 90 and was awarded the Presidential Medal of Freedom by President Barack Obama in 2012.

Potter Stewart *(1915–1985)* — Appointed by President Dwight D. Eisenhower as an associate justice in 1958, he was a pragmatic jurist and moderate presence on the Court, preferring to consider each case on its merits. As such, he was often a critical swing vote. He supported a woman's right to an abortion in *Roe v. Wade* and joined in the majority in *Furman v. Georgia*, which temporarily halted the use of the death penalty as cruel and unusual punishment. He is widely known for his opinion in *Jacobellis v. Ohio*. Referring to obscenity, he wrote, "I know it when I see it." He retired from the Court in 1981.

Joseph Story *(1779–1845)* — Appointed by President James Madison as an associate justice in 1812, he was, at 32 years old, the youngest justice appointed to the Supreme Court. He was often closely aligned with Chief Justice John Marshall in his views. Known as a preeminent legal scholar and orator, he became Dane Professor of Law at Harvard in 1829 and was a key figure in the founding of Harvard Law School. He served on the Court until his death in 1845.

George Sutherland *(1862–1942)* — Appointed by Warren G. Harding as an associate justice in 1922, he was a member of the so-called "Four Horsemen," the conservative justices who repeatedly ruled against FDR's New Deal. Over time, the Court became more amenable to New Deal legislation. Sutherland wrote the opinion of the Court in *Powell v. Alabama*, which overturned the convictions of nine young African American defendants who were convicted in hasty trials without the benefit of effective counsel. The Court held that, in capital cases, counsel must be provided to defendants as a requirement of due process. He retired in 1938.

Clarence Thomas *(b. 1948)* — Appointed by President George H. W. Bush as an associate justice in 1991, he became the second African American to sit on the Court. He was narrowly confirmed after allegations of sexual harassment surfaced and played out dramatically during his confirmation proceedings. He is a staunch conservative and an originalist, interpreting the Constitution according to its plain literal meaning at the time it was written, as well as a strong proponent of religious freedom. He is currently the longest-serving justice on the Court.

Fred M. Vinson *(1890–1953)* — Appointed by President Harry S. Truman as chief justice in 1946, he was a practical jurist inclined to defer to the other branches of government. Under his leadership, though, the Court began to view the systematic segregation of African Americans as a violation of the Equal Protection Clause. Presiding over a deeply divided Court that he was largely unable to unite, he served as chief justice until his sudden death in 1953.

Earl Warren *(1891–1974)* — Appointed by President Dwight D. Eisenhower as chief justice in 1953, he was a fierce champion of civil rights and civil liberties. He wrote the opinion of the Court in *Brown v. Board of Education*, the seminal decision that ended school segregation on the basis of race. Other landmark decisions of the Warren Court include *Miranda v. Arizona*, which outlined a protocol for informing criminal defendants of their rights, and *Loving v. Virginia*, which upheld the right of interracial couples to marry. Retired in 1969, he was posthumously awarded the Presidential Medal of Freedom by President Ronald Reagan in 1981.

Byron White *(1917–2002)* — A former professional football player, he was appointed to the Court by President John F. Kennedy. Known as a practical jurist rather than a proponent of a strict judicial philosophy, he joined the majority in cases rejecting racial discrimination and upholding voting rights, yet consistently opposed the Court's expansion of individual rights. He served as an associate justice from 1962 until 1993, and was posthumously awarded the Presidential Medal of Freedom by President George W. Bush in 2003.